MW01245435

Leadership for Such a Time as This

"If you're a leader or an aspiring one . . . and you want to find out how to become more effective and efficient in an ever-changing world, this book is for you. Drawing from personal and professional experiences as well as on a synthesis of conventional and emerging leadership theories and practices, the author skillfully integrates, in a coherent framework, some key leadership competencies that must be enhanced for a greater comparative edge in this twenty-first century's cross-cultural organizations. The 'how to do it' questions are clearly addressed and explained. This innovative study starts and ends with a call for immediate action in favor of a new style of leadership that is global and inclusive in nature so as to successfully steer and manage changes in face of complex and multidimensional challenges of our times."

—**Dr. Bruno T. Mukendi, PhD,** Professor of Strategic Leadership, CEO of the Washington International Management Institute, and Author of *Leadership and Change Management in Post-Conflict States*

"In *Leadership for Such a Time as This: A Leader's Journey to Global Inclusivity,* Dr. Mukendi covers significant ground in understanding the complexities of today's leadership climate while simultaneously taking us through his own journey and experiences that support his leadership framework. In each era, we all define what leadership is by what we tolerate, accept, and how we as leaders perform. It is a great responsibility, and I believe this book captures that. Dr. Mukendi finds a perfect balance of strong research, his own personal experiences, and powerful stories that show the power of inclusivity, working across cultures, and acknowledgment that it takes constant thought and purposeful behavior to create a culture of belonging and inclusion. Just as 'every generation is defined by a unifying cause,' every generation needs to redefine leadership that aligns with how we engage as humans and continues to enhance the cornerstone of business —an organizational culture that is its strategic competitive advantage. The culture of teams and organizations is a shadow of the leaders within it. It was refreshing to share in this journey with Dr. Mukendi's stories and leadership perspective. In times such as these, we can all explore opportunities to 'be more effective leaders at home, at work, and in our communities.'"

—**Joe Dicianno, PhD, MBA,** Director of Talent Management and Organizational Development, Adjunct Faculty at University of Pittsburgh, Author of A *Busy Leader's Guide to Caring Leadership,* and Lifelong Leadership Researcher/Scholar

"In this era where inclusivity has become an essential quality for effective leadership, Dr. Mukendi expertly captures the essence of what being a truly great leader means in his book *Leadership for Such a Time as This: A Leader's Journey to Global Inclusivity.*

"Drawing from his extensive research and personal journey across different countries in Africa and America, Dr. Mukendi has positioned himself as a prominent expert in the field of leadership studies.

"His book offers invaluable insights that will resonate with leaders across industries, scholars, and students alike. Dr. Mukendi does a fantastic job of interweaving his personal journey into his conceptualization of the global inclusive leadership framework.

"Leaders in every industry can benefit from perusing the pages of this book because it not only provides practical examples but also offers a new way to look at the responsibility of leaders.

"You will surely benefit from picking up this book!"

—**Juana Catalina** Rodriguez, Founder JnC Nova, Board Advisor and Investor, Award-Winning Author of *Unsettled Disruption*

"A must-read whether you are a leader now or in previous generations. Certainly, a manual for how our leaders today and future leaders should lead. Dr. Muteba discusses in his book the characteristics of leading in today's time. Over the last few years, the world has been challenged and lacked the leadership abilities and experiences to cope with and resolve these challenges.

"As the world evolves, there are so many more potential obstacles as it relates to artificial intelligence (AI), world peace, and being able to cope with racial and equality issues in this world. This requires a top-down and a bottom-up approach as it relates to organizational leadership and management.

"This masterpiece . . . is a road map on what today's and future leaders should focus on. . . .

"Again, I commend Dr. Muteba for his great insight and mindset on *Leadership for Such a Time as This*. This book should be on every leader's nightstand as a must-read!!"

—**Dr. James JC Cooley,** CEO and President of the JC Cooley Foundation

"I am happy to provide an endorsement for the book *Leadership for Such a Time as This: A Leader's Journey to Global Inclusivity* by Dr. Muteba Mukendi. This book is a must-read for anyone who wants to become an exceptional and a more effective leader in our increasingly diverse and interconnected world.

"Dr. Mukendi has a wealth of experience as a leader in various fields, including government, academia, and international organizations. In this book, he shares his insights on what it takes to be a successful leader in today's complex and rapidly changing global environment.

"What I appreciate most about this book is Dr. Mukendi's emphasis on inclusivity. He argues that true leadership requires a deep understanding and appreciation of the diversity of perspectives and experiences that exist in our world today. Moreover, he provides practical advice on how leaders can create a more inclusive and equitable workplace or community, and how they can leverage diversity to drive innovation and growth.

"Throughout the book, Dr. Mukendi uses real-world examples and case studies to illustrate his points, making the concepts easy to understand and apply. His writing is clear, concise, and engaging, making this book a pleasure to read.

"In summary, *Leadership for Such a Time as This* is an essential read for anyone who wants to become a more effective leader in today's rapidly changing world. Dr. Mukendi's insights and practical advice on inclusivity and diversity will help you navigate the challenges of leadership with confidence and compassion. I highly recommend this book to anyone who wants to make a positive impact in their organization or community."

—**Jean D. Francis, PhD,** Author of *Naked Truth*

Leadership for Such a Time as This:
A Leader's Journey to Global Inclusivity

by Dr. Muteba Mukendi

© Copyright 2023 Dr. Muteba Mukendi

ISBN 979-8-88824-014-4

Published by

3705 Shore Drive
Virginia Beach, VA 23455
800-435-4811
www.koehlerbooks.com

Leadership for Such a Time as This:

A LEADER'S JOURNEY TO GLOBAL INCLUSIVITY

Dr. Muteba Mukendi

VIRGINIA BEACH
CAPE CHARLES

This book was undoubtedly a labor of love;
as such, so many people
contributed with their love and support.

Dr. Candace Mukendi, my wife, my partner,
no other person is more deserving of acclaim.

Zara-Grace and Ava-Joy, my daughters,
who inspire me to be a better man and father every day.

Dr. Bruno and Etty-Bela Mukendi,
my parents, who sacrificed so much for me to
have the opportunities I've been granted.

Zephaniah, Glory, Eden, and Trezila,
my siblings, who continue to keep me grounded.

The many family members, friends, and colleagues
whose advice and prayers are invaluable.

Table of Contents

Preface | 1

Chapter 1. Introduction | 5

Chapter 2. The Value of Inclusivity | 21

Intersectional Identities | 33

Chapter 3. Meeting at the Intersection | 35

Chapter 4. Culture is Strategy.. | 50

Moral Capabilities | 63

Chapter 5. The Psychology of a Leader | 65

Chapter 6. Combating Ethical Paradoxes | 78

Chapter 7. Leadership and Motivation | 90

Intercultural Competencies | 103

Chapter 8. Building Competencies for Success | 105

Chapter 9. Global Inclusive Leadership Competency | 120

Chapter 10. Closing Thoughts and Future Considerations | 133

Appendix | 140

Bibliography | 149

Index | 164

About the Author | 166

Preface

Generally, when I share with people that I wrote a book, I'm asked three questions. Why did I write a book? What is the book about? Who is the book intended for? These three questions are critically important, so I'd like to address each one. I hope that understanding the intent behind the book will encourage you to read it in its entirety, use the resources provided, and share with others who can benefit from the book's content.

Why did I write this book? Over the last several years, I've come to appreciate leadership as a field of study. Organizational success has always been linked to effective leadership. Becoming a student of strategic leadership has helped me understand the importance of a leader's role in planning, executing, and decision-making. Over the last decade, the leader's role has evolved to much more. A leader is a futurist, a communicator, and even a creative driver. It can be an overwhelming expectation for anyone to take on all these characteristics.

It's conceivable to assume that there is a leadership theory that speaks to all our many expectations of leaders. For example, trait theory suggests leaders are born, power theory suggests positional power is essential to getting things done, and relationship theory suggests interactions with others as a key component of leadership. That is why I devoted years of research to the topic of leadership. Initially, I wanted to determine the "ideal" leadership approach for organizational success. As I came to find out, there is no such thing.

Leadership reflects the times of the day. Therefore, leadership and leadership theory continuously evolve. As the saying goes, "What worked yesterday may not work today," or "You can't do today's job with yesterday's methods." I shifted my research to focus on what leadership characteristics would be necessary to lead in this day and age. I found many candidates, such as transformational leadership or servant leadership. My research pointed to globally inclusive leadership as leadership for today. This is why I wrote *Leadership for Such a Time as This*, to provide leadership tools for our times.

Allow me to insert a parenthetical question. Why did I name this book *Leadership for Such a Time as This*? For those that are curious, I'm glad to share. The term "for such a time as this" comes from one of my favorite stories in the Bible, in Esther 4:14. The verse reads, *"And who knows whether you have not attained royalty for such a time as this?"* The protagonist, Queen Esther, has an opportunity to save her people, and in her reluctance, her uncle, Mordecai, delivers this message of encouragement. It's a call to action, and Esther takes the mantle. In her response to Mordecai, she states the famous phrase, "And if I perish, I perish." By no means should leaders require such a high calling (to place their life on the line) to accomplish their goals; however, the leadership call to action is the meaning behind the name.

What is this book about? The book introduces the global inclusive leadership framework. Based on my research and experiences, inclusive leadership provides the practical skills leaders need to lead for such a time as this. The book walks through each pillar of the framework and gives guidance on specific areas for leadership development. Each chapter will close with a global leadership imperative. This section will provide questions for leaders to consider as they take on this inclusive leadership journey. The book is also about my lived experiences as a young boy traveling from country to country. Each country provided me with a relevant leadership experience that I highlighted in the book.

This book is not meant to be a diversity, equity, and inclusion book. Although I championed several Diversity, Equity, and Inclusion (DEI) causes in my career, I wrote this book from a leadership perspective. As mentioned before, I was looking for what leadership style was required for today, and global inclusive leadership is the answer, and this book will show why. You will see many DEI topics; however, the intent was to create a book that explains how to solve our leadership challenge.

Who is the audience for this book? This book is for leaders and future leaders. There are a number of business cases and leadership implications that are helpful to leaders who are looking for ways to improve their leadership capabilities. This book will provide real-world solutions to organizational challenges even if you aren't in a leadership role. As a lifelong student of leadership, I hope this book serves the community of leadership students and the next generation of leadership scholars. I hope this helps elevate your consciousness.

CHAPTER 1.

Introduction

December 24, 1989, a day that will live in perpetual infamy. It had been nearly a year since we arrived in Liberia, a small country on the west coast of Africa. The country had entered the initial stages of civil unrest. The conflict resulted from the growing frustration of the indigenous people, who felt they didn't have a voice in the political government led by Samuel Doe, the president at the time. My family had just moved to Liberia from the United States. We were aware of the challenges the country faced, and although the threat of a government takeover was real, no one could foretell how eminent it was at the time.

It wasn't until Christmas Eve, when the rebel forces, led by Charles Taylor, crossed into Liberia from Ivory Coast, a neighboring country, that the world would understand the gravity of the situation. For my parents and other foreigners working in the capital city of Monrovia, the word came within days to leave the country until further notice. We were immediately told to flee to neighboring Senegal, presumably until the tensions would ease and we would be allowed to return. Unfortunately, that would mark the end of our time in Liberia and the beginning of the civil war.

The ethnic and class hostilities would worsen over the year, leading to a fourteen-year civil war. Liberia has historically been divided between natives and settlers. The settlers were formerly enslaved people who were repatriated to West Africa between the early 1820s through 1867. Eventually, the two groups would clash, intensifying ethnic division and causing leaders to abuse their power. A population-based survey administered by the University of Berkeley's Human Rights Center reported that the war's leading root causes were corruption, tribal and ethnic identity issues, poverty, and inequality. The respondents were also asked whom they believed was responsible for the conflict, and over 70 percent blamed the leaders, Taylor and Doe.[1]

The Liberian challenge serves as a business case for *global inclusive leadership* (GIL), a leadership concept that recognizes the value of cross-cultural integration. My personal experience in Liberia and other countries sparked enough interest in me to explore other best practices for developing leaders who can drive and sustain inclusionary efforts. Given my consulting and other work experience spanning different continents, I wanted to understand how such concepts could be applied to a larger ecosystem, at national or even global levels, in government, for-profit and not-for-profit, and small or large teams.

I've always considered myself somewhat of a global citizen. Having had the great fortune to grow up, visit, and work in several continents, I've always appreciated having a global perspective. Like most of us, my experiences have helped shape who I am. Although the journey to be an inclusive leader has been a long, never-ending road of learning, there are several events I can point to that led to my philosophical construct on global inclusion that I'll expound on in this

---

1. Vinck, Pham, and Kreutzer, "Talking Peace: A Population-Based Survey on Attitudes About Security, Dispute Resolution, and Post-Conflict Reconstruction in Liberia."

book. Over the years, I integrated practical knowledge and wisdom about inclusion into my research on leadership as I delved deeper into the changes occurring in the world that brought a convergence between both fields of study.

Leadership Today

Leadership was and always is at the center of any significant global crisis. According to The Listening Project, a BBC program, in a survey of over 30,000 adults across the globe, there is a critical global leadership crisis. This report points to financial vulnerability, access and affordability of education, corruption, and lack of transparency as leading causes of the crisis.[2] Undoubtedly, the COVID-19 pandemic has amplified the world's public health and socioeconomic challenges. The survey, which was done originally in February 2020, then again in September 2020 to account for the impact of the coronavirus, also showed how issues that were once siloed are now interdependent. For example, income inequality is uniquely linked to access to affordable healthcare; access to the internet is linked to education. Figure 1.1 shows the areas of interdependence from disease prevention to political freedoms and social justice.

A survey published by the World Economic Forum, the foundation focused on improving the global agenda, found that 86 percent of respondents agree that there is a leadership crisis in the world today.[3] Lastly, in 2016, a Gallup poll reported that, of the 35,000 leaders surveyed, 82 percent of managers aren't very good at leading people.

---

2. Milken Institute and The Harris Poll, "Global Priorities According to Global Citizens."

3. "Why the World in 2015 Faces a Leadership Crisis."

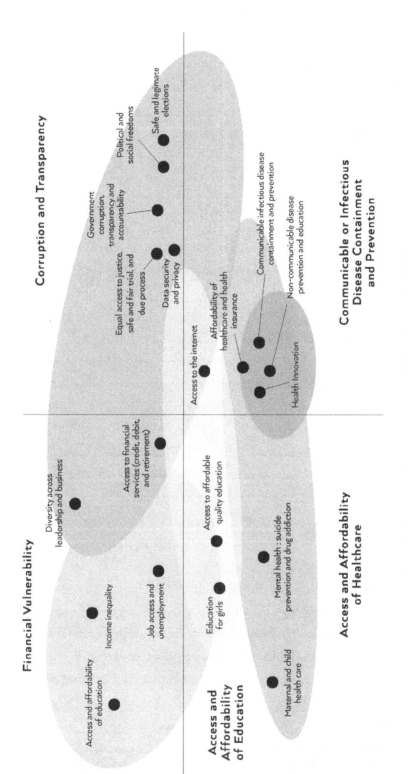

Figure 1.1. Reasons and Interdependence of Global Leadership Crisis

In the US, this lack of leadership capabilities costs organizations $550 billion annually.[4] Several recent global and regional events reinforce the importance of leadership development. In 2020 alone, not only did we grapple with a global pandemic but also a race and social justice movement, an economic crisis, a politically polarized election, and an attack on the US Capitol Building. Some point to leaders who exacerbated these challenges rather than bringing solutions to the table. Leadership surely remains of pivotal importance; global inclusive leadership can be the difference between addressing challenges to create solutions and creating an environment doomed for utter failure.

Given these surveys as context, I suggest integrating inclusion into leadership practices to help bridge the leadership gap. Through a series of fact-based research and autobiographical accounts and recollections, I'll take you on a journey to uncover inclusive leadership insights. The goal is to identify and draw lessons on how this innovative leadership approach can bring about personal, organizational, and societal change.

Global Leadership for Such a Time as This

Some may ask, "Why Leadership? Have there not been enough books written about leadership?" Leadership is undoubtedly one of the most intriguing topics of our times. A Google Scholar search returns nearly five million results on the discipline. The sheer amount of empirical and theoretical leadership studies point to its critical nature. And

---

4. Hougaard and Carter, *The Mind of the Leader: How to Lead Yourself, Your People, and Your Organization for Extraordinary Results*

if you're anything like me and have read through several leadership books, you may wonder, *What else is there to learn?* I assure you, our ever-changing world creates the need for constant reinvention. For decades, scholars have questioned theories, methods, and approaches to the leadership challenge. At the center of this debate is the perception that leadership concepts are evolving, and thus we continue to ask the same questions. *What is the correct form of leadership, if any? How does one gain leadership skills? Is it truly learned, or are their innate qualities that reside in so-called "good leaders"? What makes an "effective" leader in a changing world? And lastly, how can one improve leadership skills?*

Throughout my life, I've encountered and learned from many different leaders. One lesson that persists in all my interactions is that nothing lasts forever. Leadership is no different. If you're curious about the future of leadership—using the global inclusive framework—this book will help give meaning to the "what" and the "how" concerning leadership. Before defining GIL, let's review a few trends highlighting the leadership challenge.

Trend #1: Increased Inclination to "Go Global"

Globalization is a significant factor in shifting the needle on leadership performance. For decades, organizations have profited from the wave of globalization. Globalization has shifted workforces from one nation to another, where a lower-cost model could be implemented. Globalization has also improved the sourcing and supply chain of materials and amplified the need for technology and innovation across multiple sectors. The recent Regional Comprehensive Economic Partnership (RCEP) in the Asia-Pacific region, United States-Mexico-

Canada Agreement (USMCA), and African Continental Free Trade Area (AfCFTA) were all signed with the intent to open regional markers.[5] Globalization isn't going anywhere; this trend will continue for years to come.

Trend #2: Changing Operational Models

As you read this book, the world is going through a shift. The impact of the COVID-19 pandemic will likely continue to demand changes in how organizations work. The Future of Work scholars point to this shift as contributing to rebuilding the fundamentals of humanity.[6] Changes in how we now work demand changes in how we now lead. A Future of Work study by Accenture revealed that, of the nearly 10,000 workers surveyed, 83 percent said they prefer a hybrid model.[7] Most organizations have plans to move to either a hybrid or an entirely remote model. Ford, Citigroup, Target, and Microsoft are a few examples of organizations moving to a hybrid model, and more are following.[8] However, a number of traditional workforce strategies require in-person staff. As organizations take on efforts to determine which activities do not require in-person presence, they will likely move the operations to align with the trend. For global leaders, approaches to leadership will change due in part to managing remote and hybrid teams.

5. Altman and Bastian, "The State of Globalization in 2021.

6. Antonacopoulou and Georgiadou, "Leading through Social Distancing: The Future of Work, Corporations and Leadership from Home."

7. "The Future of Work: A Hybrid Work Model."

8. Carino, "Companies Moving to Hybrid Workplaces Will Face New Challenges.

Trend #3: Improved Automation
Capabilities Across Borders

Implementing new technologies expedites the need for knowledge professionals to change their functions. The advent of technology puts pressure on organizations to think strategically about transitioning to the changing environment.[9] Functions like finance and human resources will focus on customer service, collaboration, and business partnering.[10] Workers will shift to roles where they will provide more advice on a strategic intervention based on the insights derived from the innovative tools at their disposal. Employees will become "digital assistants" with a high aptitude for technical literacy who can create visualizations and present solutions to business partners. Leaders will not only contend with the workplace changing but also the work itself. Leaders will not only contend with the workplace changing but also the work itself, especially with the advent of artificial intelligence tools such as manufacturing robots, machine learning in financial investment, and marketing chatbots. Global leaders will focus on developing team members to support new organizational roles and responsibilities.

Global Leadership

James MacGregor Burns, a well-known historian and grandfather of leadership studies, said, "Leadership is one of the most observed and least understood phenomena on earth." This statement was always

---

9. Marsh, McAllum, and Purcell, *Strategic Foresight: The Power of Standing in the Future.*

10. Sher and Englert, "Finance Digital Transformation: Predictions for 2025."

perplexing, but it is entirely accurate. Leadership means something different in different contexts. In its most basic form, leadership is defined as a process whereby an individual influences a group of individuals to achieve a common goal.[11] This definition highlights the contrast leadership provides as a two-party process between a leader and follower(s). Each plays its own role; the leader drives the vision, engages the audience, and makes tough decisions.

In comparison, the follower's story is rarely told outside of the leader's influence on their performance. Essentially, the leader provides guidance based on a series of interactions with followers, and the follower, in most situations, acquiesces to the needs. There is a big gap in research on followership. Follower development is not as practical as that of leaders. During the COVID-19 pandemic, for example, the workforce underwent a transition as people left their jobs, opting to move into roles unlike the conventional nine-to-five. Professor Anthony Klotz recently coined the term "The Great Resignation" to illustrate the pandemic's impact on people's well-being.[12] Even more recently, the term "quiet quitting" has emerged to define employees who avoid going above and beyond and thus do the bare minimum.[13] Employees are increasingly driven by job satisfaction and overall gratification. Given this context, it's even more critical that we double down on developing leaders of the future who understand employees' motivations. Solving tomorrow's problems will require leaders to develop other leaders, no longer looking at them as mere followers but rather emphasizing the need to cultivate social characteristics and behaviors that effectively create change.

---

11. Northouse, Leadership: Theory and Practice.

12. Borenstein, "Three Indisputable Truths About the Great Resignation."

13. Tapper, "Quiet Quitting: Why Doing the Bare Minimum at Work Has Gone Global."

Global leadership is different from traditional leadership. For one, the global context makes the leadership task more complex. Cultural challenges are amplified, ethical dilemmas are more frequent, and cross-border tensions are front and center. Therefore, when defining global leadership, all these complexities must be considered. Over the years, many definitions have focused on the global reach of leadership, figuratively adding the word "global" to a contemporary definition of leadership. Some scholars define the global leader as an executive who sits in a role that involves some degree of international scope.[14] Others explain the global leader as anyone who leads global change efforts in public, private, or nonprofit sectors.[15] There are elements of these definitions that reign true for every global leader. However, the definition must encompass the wide-ranging characteristics of the global context. Simply including the word "global" in a signature line or business card does not make one a global leader.

In the article "Defining the 'global' in global leadership," the authors sought to unify the plethora of existing definitions around global leadership. They concluded, "Global leaders are individuals who effect significant positive change in organizations by building communities through the development of trust and the arrangement of organizational structures and processes in a context involving multiple cross-boundary stakeholders, multiple sources of external cross-boundary authority, and multiple cultures under conditions of temporal, geographical, and cultural complexity."[16] This description provides a thorough characterization of the current global leader.

---

14. Spreitzer, McCall, and Mahoney, "Early Identification of International Executive Potential."

15. Osland, "An Overview of the Global Leadership Literature.

16. Mendenhall et al., "Defining the 'Global' in Global Leadership

Nevertheless, the global leader of the future will have increased pressure to balance organizational needs and the needs of all stakeholders.

Inclusive Leadership

Inclusion is a well-known concept in most workplaces today. At this point, there aren't many companies that haven't responded to the call for inclusive working environments to some degree. It involves this notion that leaders display skills related to inclusive practice in the workplace to change and create an inclusive environment where employees' needs for belongingness and uniqueness are satisfied.[17] Queinetta M. Roberson, the author of "Disentangling the Meanings of Diversity and Inclusion in Organizations," defined inclusion as "the removal of obstacles to the full participation and contribution of employees in organizations."[18] This definition accurately labels inclusion as a method for breaking down barriers that promote segregation and marginalization in society.

Inclusive behaviors include empathy and self-awareness to drive engagement and retention in the workplace. Inclusion is a leadership concept but also an organizational imperative. In global ecosystems where mental health and well-being are becoming top priorities and hiring diverse talent is a must, inclusion is quickly becoming part of the formula for success. Historically, organizations have relied on their team leaders to establish norms and ways of working to "get the job done." However, such a management approach is never foolproof if inclusive practices are not integrated into the culture and strategy.

---

17. Shore et al., "Inclusion and Diversity in Work Groups: A Review and Model for Future Research.

18. Roberson, "Disentangling the Meanings of Diversity and Inclusion in Organizations."

It's amazing how often organizations still miss this simple fact: every goal, tactic, or approach must be aligned to effectively promote inclusion. For example, having a goal to recruit a higher percentage of minorities is achievable. However, the only way to retain minority groups includes setting up internal mechanisms, like training and mentoring programs to promote growth and retention. Additionally, depending on where in the world you live, further resources may be needed to promote inclusionary practices, such as ensuring adequate infrastructure, contributing to policy development, and creating partnerships with local organizations to support community programs.

Global Inclusive Leadership

Global inclusive leadership (GIL) was birthed from the idea that organizations are going through a shift. This shift will require focusing on being the best *for* the world rather than being the best *in* the world. What drives us can no longer amount to merely representing the interest of shareholders but rather all direct and indirect stakeholders. The organizational purpose should permeate through structural walls, putting emphasis on what truly matters—the people. To be globally inclusive, leaders influence a wide range of players; thus, their decisions must be influenced by employees, contractors, suppliers, vendors, and the community. Therefore, this type of leadership requires merging two schools of thought on global and inclusive leadership.

I want to challenge the implication that global inclusive leadership is just leadership from afar or that it's solely dependent on cross-border interactions. Global inclusive leadership starts at home and in local communities. It's more about connecting the dots across the board.

How does a decision to close a factory in Baltimore, Maryland, impact the parts suppliers in Bangladesh? How does a local human resource policy impact employee group dynamics in foreign countries? What's the environmental impact of the air quality on the community? These questions are critical issues that leaders should think through before making decisions. There are many characteristics of leadership, global inclusive leadership, however, is primarily concerned with leadership behavior, how behavior impacts decision-making." In this book, I emphasize GIL as a framework for advancing practical leadership behaviors for the twenty-first century.

The Global Inclusive Leadership Framework

The global inclusive leader drives change by building a globally connected environment where all internal and external stakeholders

Figure 1.2. Global Inclusive Leadership Framework

benefit from the structure and processes put in place. The GIL framework has three central attributes: intersectional identities, moral capacities, and intercultural competencies. Figure 1.2 describes each attribute in the framework.

The three components are based on a me-us-now framework in storytelling.[19] The framework explains how storytelling first starts with talking about "me." In this phase, storytellers share lived experiences that help to connect the audience through stories and anecdotes. Then, the story of "me" evolves into the story of "us," where a collective audience is brought into the story, helping them to feel part of and tied to the speaker's plot. Lastly, the "now" tells the story of the *how* and the *what*. The "now" tells everyone why the story matters and how they can get involved. It's the call to action that brings that whole story to fruition. Let's dive deeper into each phase.

Me

Intersectional identities and intersectionality are concepts through which one acknowledges the intersections of identities in each person's life. The story I shared at the beginning of this chapter is a glimpse into how the Global Inclusive Leadership Framework can support leaders in their quest to bring people and teams together. Global inclusive leaders are first, before anything, self-aware.[20] This self-awareness trait contributes to building an individual's moral compass, trust, integrity, honesty, and purpose. Self-awareness allows leaders to be their "true" selves and bring followers on a journey of self-discovery. This awareness can ultimately lead to authentic

19. Shiftbalance, "The Story of Me, Us, Now."

20. Sosik and Jung, *Full Range Leadership Development: Pathways for People, Profit, and Planet*

behavior. Authenticity requires opening up and sharing about oneself. There is no need to act like someone other than yourself when you are authentic. Sharing your values can work in your favor and create the basis for strong relationships. Furthermore, trust is established through this social exchange.[21] It all starts with knowing who you are in the context of those in your circle.

Us

Morality is a crucial component of leadership. Joanne Ciulla, a renowned scholar on ethical leadership, expounded that superior leadership requires technical competence and moral capacity.[22] Moral leaders are those that lead with a moral compass. The metaphorical compass is made up of a series of values that leaders collect throughout their lives.[23] As a matter of fact, we all possess moral values that help us make decisions every day. Therefore, our behavior is largely dependent on our internal moral code. GIL requires leaders who lead with moral authority. Defining moral authority is a challenge, especially when we scale the term at the global level. Moral values can be different in different cultures and geographic regions. Organizational morality is built on a shared view. To assess moral competence, we can only compare relative to another organization. However, all stakeholders should contribute to assessing a leader's moral standard.

---

21. Engelbrecht, Heine, and Mahembe, "Integrity, Ethical Leadership, Trust and Work Engagement."

22. Ciulla, "Leadership Ethics: Mapping the Territory."

23. Sendjaya, "Morality and Leadership: Examining the Ethics of Transformational Leadership.

Now

Intercultural competencies are about acquiring the skills to drive global inclusive action. The global inclusive leader does not evade accountability, does not accept the "survival of the fittest" pressures of business, and does not release anyone from the responsibility to respect another's dignity and humanity.[24] They can connect the dots, see their decisions' impact, and react accordingly. Furthermore, this leader understands that they represent more than just the shareholders' interests. Their reach extends beyond the organization's walls to stakeholders in all channels. In order to fulfill this mandate, this leader understands the need for continuous education to improve the organizational structure and culture.

I invite you to take this journey of exploration with me to learn more about the global inclusive leadership framework.

---

24. Costa, *The Ethical Imperative: Why Moral Leadership Is Good Business.*

CHAPTER 2

The Value of Inclusivity

The Outsider, the Only, and the Other

Before diving into the importance of inclusivity, let's first unpack the meaning of inclusion's antonym: exclusion. In my experience, you can't accurately comprehend what it means to be an inclusive leader if you have never felt excluded. Exclusion, from the perspective of the individual being excluded, generally takes on three characteristics: the "outsider," the "only," or the "other." If you've been part of an exclusive group or club, you understand the privilege that comes with such a membership. An *outsider* is one who is denied access to participate or engage in a group. On the other hand, an *only* is one who has access but lacks common representation. If you've been in a room where you were visibly the only one of a particular identity, you likely experienced what it feels like to be the *only*. The *other* is one who has access and may have common representation; however, they find themselves defined by the represented group instead of their own volitions. If you've fallen victim to a stereotype—maybe someone's unconscious bias got the best of you—you likely experienced being the *other*.

At different points in my life, I've embodied one of the three *O*s.

From a young age, I knew I was different. My name would be the first thing to give it away. I recall being in elementary school and dreading the moment when any teacher would call my name during roll call. I would start to shrink in my seat as I watched my teacher's face frown, trying to figure out how to enunciate what must have seemed like random letters thrown together.

The teacher would incorrectly state my name, "Muuuuteeee-mmmmbbaaaa?" and look up with a curious gaze. The whole class would join in on the curiosity, looking to see who would respond. "Here," I would reply with a quivery voice, too afraid to correct the mispronunciation, not to mention the additional letters added to my name. In the 1980s, being a second-generation American was still a novelty. I was the odd kid with the weird name. Strangely enough, being the weird kid, other kids would treat me one of two ways. I was either met with extreme interest or extreme reservation. It meant that people treated me nicely or coldly because of the novelty of being different. I was a quiet kid who was generally okay with having this polarizing presence. I was content with my very small group of friends, most of whom grew up with similar experiences. Even more significantly, I was aware of my foes, the ones who laughed at my expense. Being the outsider was never particularly appealing; I had the same desire to be included that any young kid would—the desire to fit in.

As an outsider, I did my best to blend in, doing nothing that would raise unnecessary attention. Assimilation is a very common attribute of an outsider. In Trevor Noah's book *Born a Crime*, he explains, "It is easier to be an insider as an outsider than to be an outsider as an insider. . . . You will face more hate and ridicule and ostracism than you can even begin to fathom. People are willing to accept you if they see you as an outsider trying to assimilate into their world. But when they see you as a fellow tribe member attempting to disavow the tribe, that is something they will never forgive." This was my story. I was the same yet different. I was in a classroom but still in a room of my own.

Growing up as an outsider made me increasingly aware of my surroundings. I would go through an internal discourse to determine how certain interactions would play out. Based on my initial assessment—their look, what they wore, their behavior—I could make up my own assumptions of the outcome. For example, my inner voice would utter, "That person seems like someone nice I can talk to," or "Hmm, that person is someone who won't get along with me." Admittedly, most of my judgment may have been incorrect, but that didn't stop me one bit. Being the outsider helped build a wall of my own creation, a version of the story I believed to be true. In my discussions with friends, this is where a lot of people who feel excluded get stuck; they build that wall, and it becomes a challenge to tear it down.

I would eventually learn how to manage the so-called "outsider syndrome" only to find myself entering the realm of the *only*. Throughout my professional career, there have been several times when I found myself to be the only one with a specific identity. At times, I was the only Black man (or one of just a few) in a predominantly White office. At other times, I was the guy with the name few dared to pronounce, and therefore I was called upon infrequently for my input. Even more simply, I was the introvert in a room of extroverted people. I found more resilience in every situation as time went on, and eventually, I learned how to respond or not respond in some cases. However, in a few cases, being the only one is best solved in time. Over time, I went from being the *only* to welcoming others like me through the recruitment process. However, recruiting is a much more straightforward undertaking compared to the challenges of retaining a diverse workforce.

One challenge with retention is managing environments where people feel like the *other*. I've seldomly dealt with this personally, but in my interactions with several colleagues, this continues to challenge organizations. Generally, implicit or unconscious bias is the root cause; however, there may be other underlying factors. We all harbor some degree of unconscious bias. Most times, the impact is harmless, but other times, the impact is disastrous. A colleague once shared a story of the challenges she experienced in an organization she had recently joined. As background, she has a Ph.D. and over fifteen years of experience in her field. She was a highly touted professional. However, coming into this new environment proved stressful. She was excluded from several career-advancing opportunities. She eventually discovered that despite her many accolades, she was stereotyped as a young Black woman.

Feeling like an *outsider*, an *only*, or an *other* is common in the corporate and public sectors. Women in leadership, for example, have fallen prey to *outsider syndrome*. Although women may be more educated and, at times, more experienced than their male counterparts, they are "left out of the club." Ultimately, not fitting in and lacking social networks and relationships can lead to isolation.[25] Isolation can also lead to another phenomenon called *imposter syndrome*. It refers to employees feeling like frauds despite ending up in well-regarded roles and positions. Impostor feelings are often linked to marginalized groups in society; to date, research mainly points to this syndrome as an individual issue.[26] Imposter syndrome can cause negative stress, intense fear of failure, anxiety, loss of confidence, and eventually derailment.[27]

---

25. Cormier, "Why Top Professional Women Still Feel like Outsiders."

26. Feenstra et al., "Contextualizing the Impostor 'Syndrome.'"

27. Mount and Tardanico, Beating the Impostor Syndrome.

Isolation can lead to several personal and organizational impacts if inclusionary principles are not implemented. Isolation creates structural silos and individual barriers that permeate the workplace. Overcoming feelings of isolation requires strategies to integrate into "the club" or, even better, dissolve "the club" altogether, creating a space where everyone feels included. In this new anti-club environment, not only does everyone feel included, but they also feel a sense of belonging.

Belonging

Years ago, I worked as a youth leader in my church. I spent some of my best days with those young men and women; I was inspired by the next generation of leaders. In conversations at the time, I found that many of those young adults dealt with feelings of exclusion and isolation. Most of their feelings were based on their experiences at school, dealing with their peers. As someone who has dealt with the same, those feelings were ones I knew how to address. Although I wouldn't realize this until much later in life, that isolation further amplifies the need for belonging. Those young ones needed a space where they could feel like they belonged, and that social environment was fostered in the youth group. We created a utopian world, a genuinely inclusive group where everyone felt part of something meaningful.

Belonging is defined as a close or intimate relationship or a sense of social connection.[28] Belonging is synonymous with kinship and personal ties. Especially at a young age, feelings of love and belonging need to be satisfied for development into adulthood. In

---

28. Baumeister and Leary, "The Need to Belong: Desire for Interpersonal Attachments as a Fundamental Human Motivation.

1943, Abraham Maslow's hierarchy of needs provided the basis for human motivation. The theory is comprised of five hierarchical stages: physiological, safety, esteem, self-actualization, and love and belonging. Figure 2.1 below represents the five-stage model. After physiological and safety needs in the pyramid-like structure comes love and belonging, where interpersonal relationships are drivers of behavior. Interpersonal relationships are the precursor to strong social connections that, if developed, can, over time, develop friendships, improve trust, and allow for affiliation to a group.[29] That sense of connection is a central building block in the hierarchy of needs. Simply said, we need to feel like we belong.

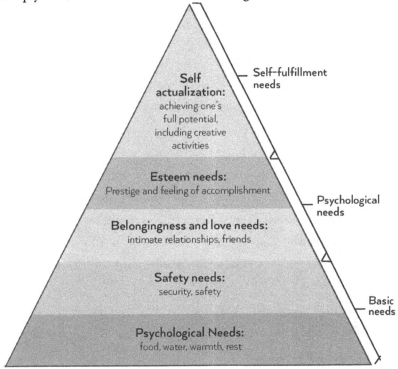

Figure 2.1. Maslow's Hierarchy of Needs

29. McLeod, "Maslow's Hierarchy of Needs."

If belonging is that simple, why is creating this sense of belonging in the workplace still an anomaly? For one, social support buffers are not built into the fabric of most organizations. Social support buffers act as a protective mechanism. For example, organizations that create programs to ensure team members can call out workplace bullying have created social support buffers.[30] Secondly, some members of minority communities may find challenges in developing social bonds in the workplace. This state is called *belonging uncertainty*, social uncertainty that leads to challenges with belonging. Belonging uncertainty is a global challenge; everyone seeks to uncover the quality of their social connections.[31] Overcoming belonging uncertainty is also a matter of adopting integrative management principles at all levels of an organization.

The Global Inclusive Leadership Imperative

Integration is a component of inclusion that we will further explore in this book. For now, suffice it to say that integration opens the door for conversation and reconciliation. As a global inclusive leader, here are a few questions to ensure *outsiders, onlys,* or *others* transition to feelings of belonging:

1. Who may feel like an outsider, an only, or an other on my team?

2. What are the signs that an outsider, an only, or an other might be in your organization?

---

30. Nielsen et al., "Workplace Bullying, Mental Distress, and Sickness Absence: The Protective Role of Social Support."

31. Walton and Cohen, "A Question of Belonging: Race, Social Fit, and Achievement."

3. How can an *outsider*, an *only*, or an *other* be integrated into the club?

4. Why might the outsiders feel like outsiders? What are the triggers?

5. Are there members of the club who exhibit behaviors that contribute to outsiders being outsiders?

6. What timeline should be considered to integrate outsiders? (If this answer is more than a month, short- to medium-term goals should be put in place.)

7. What are the benefits that will be realized because of integration?

The response to these questions can undoubtedly uncover gaps that contribute to exclusive environments. Let's consider further how this looks in practice.

The Shift

In 1988, my family moved from the United States to Liberia, a country located in West Africa. After my father completed his PhD program at the University of Pittsburgh, he was hired by the United Nations Development Programme (UNDP) as a technical advisor. The first mission was in Monrovia, the capital city. The trip was an opportunity for my dad to fulfill a lifelong goal of contributing to Africa's development efforts. For me, it was a new and fresh start where I would make new friends and, hopefully, seamlessly fit into this new environment. Don't get me wrong; I'm forever grateful for my family. As a child, I could always turn to the loving arms of my parents and siblings to satisfy the need for social belonging. However, this move was the chance to build the friendships I very much desired. I had no idea what I was walking into, but I was confident I was not leaving anything significant behind.

Little did I know, we arrived in Liberia during the country's initial stages of civil unrest. Over the years, the frustration of the indigenous people had mounted; they felt voiceless toward a political machine built on a hierarchical caste system. In this system, first came the light-skinned Americo-Liberians (people of mixed Black and White ancestry), then the dark-skinned Americo-Liberians (laborers), the recaptives or Congos (Africans who had been rescued by the US Navy while aboard US-bound slave ships and brought to Liberia), and finally, the indigenous African Liberians. Over time, all the free enslaved people migrated into one group, the Americo-Liberians or the Congos. Despite representing only 3 percent of the population, this group would control the country's economic, social, and political aspects.[32]

When we landed in the capital city of Monrovia, I was immediately captivated and overtaken with curiosity. Before arriving, I tried to learn as much as possible about the country. I'd asked my parents about the unchartered land, but I had no idea what to expect. I was immediately in love; the people, the culture, the food—it was better than I expected. We lived in a gated, one-story, semidetached house less than a mile from a beach strip that ran parallel to the Atlantic Ocean. The scene was strikingly different from the little rowhouse we left in Pittsburgh, PA. I noticed the guard who opened the gate every time we came and left. When he left, a nightguard would replace him without us even noticing. We had a maid who cleaned up after us,

---

32. Dennis, "A Brief History of Liberia."

and when my mother was pregnant, she would cook for us as well. To my siblings and me, the most exciting aspect was having a driver, an individual assigned to our family from the UN to drive us from place to place. What was not to love?

Even at a young age, I could see the signs that things weren't quite right. Liberia has a long-standing history as the first African nation to declare its independence. However, the ethnic clash was evident. I remember seeing Samuel Doe on the news, the country's president at the time. He was a rather chubby man with a thick afro and equally thick glasses. At the time, I knew little about his past, so every derogatory insinuation I saw about him seemed somehow untrue. However, his story is significant to the story of the Liberian struggle. Doe was the leader of the coup d'état that led to the death of William Tolbert, the president prior to Doe. Tolbert, a member of the America-Liberian caste, was a wealthy man whose family had a majority stake in the rice industry. His government attempted to raise the price of rice, a move that was met with much resistance from the opposition, who believed it only stood to provide wealth to Tolbert's family. Doe, a member of the indigenous caste, would order the public execution of Tolbert and his cabinet members.

Doe assumed the presidency after Tolbert's death. He had no formal leadership or political training, which challenged his ability to lead at the highest level. When members of his party put his leadership in question, his response was to execute them as well. Eventually, his cabinet would be made up primarily of members of his ethnic group. These appointments would lead to his downfall in the end. A few of his colleagues who held significant roles in the People's Redemption Council (PRC), the party headed by Doe, eventually left the country to plot a takeover. Most notably, Charles Taylor and Prince Johnson became the major threats to Doe's seat. Taylor and Johnson, both from different ethnic groups, would make plans to overthrow Doe.

Taylor and his rebel army entered the country limits of Liberia. The threat of an impending civil war sent shockwaves throughout the country. However, the government downplayed the situation. We were told this threat would eventually pass, the government would remain in total control, and the army would manage to hold off the rebel forces. December 24, 1989, marked the beginning of the end for Doe. In what seemed like the blink of an eye, he was eventually captured, tortured, and killed, much like the punishment he inflicted on Tolbert nearly ten years prior. Our family, and most other US and European foreigners, were forced to flee from our homes. Most families had little time to plan and thus sought refuge in neighboring countries. We relocated to Senegal while waiting for things to calm down and for a sign to return. The ethnic and class hostilities worsened over the year, leading to a civil war lasting fourteen years.

As researchers identified the root cause of the Liberian conflict, ethnic animosity is cited as a significant contributor. However, leadership is a critical component of economic and political instability. Whether it was Doe, Tolbert, or Taylor, they were all leaders who focused on doing what was "right" for themselves and their ethnic groups. Even if they had some honorable intentions, they carried out their objectives without much consideration for the impact those decisions would have on the country.

Let's roll back the clock to when William Tolbert was president. I wonder what would have happened if the indigenous people of Liberia felt like they had representation in the social and political arena. What if Samuel Doe or another leader of the native population was brought to the table to help address the group's challenges, and solutions were discussed to prevent future disputes? Now, I believe that some intervention methods might have been attempted at the time; however, I am emphasizing how leaders can help prevent *outsiders, onlys*, or *others* from feeling like they don't matter. I also understand these issues were likely very complex, and I am drawing a rather simplistic model, but I hope you follow the logic. When people feel disenfranchised, they can become a negative antibody to the success of any organization's goals. The Liberian case is ideal for why leaders should value inclusivity.

Let's explore how global inclusive leadership can support inclusivity by uncovering the point of intersections.

Intersectional Identities

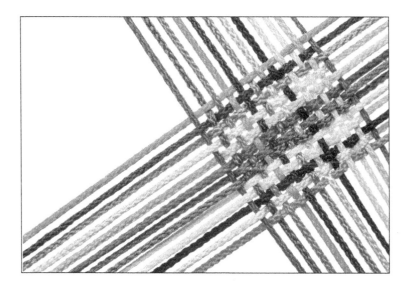

CHAPTER 3.

Meeting at the Intersection

After we absconded from Monrovia, we lived in Senegal for nearly six months. Initially, we anticipated the return to Monrovia would be imminent. Therefore, there was no perceived value in permanently relocating because, soon enough, as many believed, the war would be over. Everything changed when we received news that our house had been raided and stripped to the walls. There was no coming back, and everything we thought we would return to was in rubble. Return to Liberia was futile; we had to move on.

Living in Dakar, the capital city of Senegal, was a vastly different experience from Monrovia. Monrovia had already proven to be a significantly drastic change for kids who had spent most of their lives in Pittsburgh. In Monrovia, we experienced for the first time a school population made up of predominantly Black Africans. While we had the same skin tone, we were the ones who appeared to be different. Our accents, our mannerisms, and even our nonverbal communication brought, at times, an unwelcome spotlight on our lives. Monrovia was already a major cultural shift, but at least English was the official language. The language factor made our interactions with others less distressing.

By contrast, in Senegal, the official language is French. My parents spoke French and hoped their children would eventually do the same. In Monrovia, we had an after-school tutor who taught us French. Learning French was not my favorite activity; however, I would find myself retaining a word here and there. In Dakar, we didn't have the advantage of a tutor; we had no choice but to learn the language. We quickly picked up French and a little Wolof, another widely spoken language in Senegal. "*Na nga def?*"—"How are you?"—a passerby would ask. "*Maa ngi fi*"—"I'm fine"—we would respond confidently, knowing that we had given a proper response. I enjoyed this field-dependent style of learning and being exposed to the everyday experience.

We eventually started learning the culture as well. Unlike the secluded home we cherished in Monrovia, in Dakar, we lived in an apartment complex. It felt like we were in the center of the action. No longer living in the outskirts, we were entranced in the busiest area of the capital. From hearing the many local languages, smelling the well-seasoned grilled fish, and walking through the outdoor markets, Dakar was the perfect depiction of a culturally rich environment. Not too far away from the capital, tourists flocked to the island of Gorée, the largest slave-trading center from the fifteenth to nineteenth centuries. Although the French colonized Dakar, this island was ruled by many, including the Portuguese, Dutch, and English. Our visit there left lasting memories of human exploitation that still manifest in different ways.

I was so fascinated by Senegalese culture, particularly its many religions. I remember the first time I heard the call to prayer coming from the nearby mosque, the Grande Mosqée de Dakar. In Islam, this action signaled to the Muslim community the times to pray five times a day. It was not unusual to see people walking around with their prayer rugs, and at the sound of the blaring chimes, they would

MEETING AT THE INTERSECTION

immediately assume the position of prayer. Hearing the call, I would run to the apartment window to see if anyone was praying outside our dwelling. And if there was someone there, I would marvel at this practice, partly because I had never seen such open prayer. Another part of me was curious to see if they would ever break character during a prayer; they never did.

Another landmark, the Cathedral of Dakar, stood less than two kilometers from the mosque. At the time, I was less interested in the breathtaking Sudanese-style towers and the jaw-dropping dome structure and more captivated by the adjacent playground. We looked forward to two activities every weekend: going to the city center to ride the bumper cars and going to that playground. My parents would take us there and sit on the bench while my sister, brother, and I would have the time of our lives.

My experience in Senegal helped me understand some of the citizens' experiences, their history, and what made them who they are. Senegal is predominately Muslim, with Roman Catholic being a small percentage of the population, roughly 4.1 percent.[33] The French brought Catholicism during colonization, contributing to policies that drove cultural assimilation in the country. What made the Senegalese so perplexing was that despite the oppression they faced through colonial domination, they found so many ways to preserve their culture. Although Senegal and many of the countries I would eventually visit were not perfect, there was so much richness in their art, music, food, and values.

Looking back, I now realize that we lived at the crossroads between a mosque and a cathedral, at the junction of a buzzing urbanite town saturated with traditional and longstanding values, and at the intersection of a tourist hotbed, a town wrestling with its colonial

---

33. "Senegal - The World Factbook."

past. Intersections help bring contrasting concepts and identities together, for better or worse. Similarly, leaders must consider how these contrasts impact relationships. In this chapter, we'll explore how leaders can recognize points of intersections.

From Intersectionality to Intersecting Identities

The term intersectionality has garnished a great deal of attention since it was introduced in the late 1980s. It was first coined by the Black feminist and legal scholar Kimberle Crenshaw as a tool to contrast the multidimensionality of Black women's experiences.[34] She argued that by looking at Black women in this narrow window, without consideration for the "multiply-burdened" claims that persist in this community, we create a culture where these members are marginalized. As a result, Crenshaw believed that the experiences of Black women were excluded from the race and gender policy and theory, amplifying the need for intersectional considerations. For example, sex and race discrimination has been historically defined by the experiences of White women and Black men. She suggested that failure to account for intersectional experiences can result in a compounding effect of multiple types of discrimination and injustice toward Black women.[31]

More recently, intersectionality has become a buzzword as corporate diversity culture and identity politics have transformed the term into a more generic connotation. This label takes intersectionality outside the original context of Black women and extends it to other individuals, mainly White women's experiences of oppression.[35]

---

34 Crenshaw, "Demarginalizing the Intersection of Race and Sex: A Black Feminist Critique of Antidiscrimination Doctrine, Feminist Theory, and Antiracist Politics [1989]."

35 Davis, "Makes a Feminist Theory Successful Intersectionality as Buzzword: A Sociology of Science Perspective on What."

As intersectionality became increasingly mainstream, much of the ideologies of Black female oppression had seemingly been forgotten.[36] Similar to leadership studies, intersectionality is still in its infancy.[37] As a discipline, it has taken many different definitions over the years as scholars attempt to provide an agreed-upon characterization.

Crenshaw's research has done so much to advocate for intersectionality as a field of study. Intersectionality has evolved to represent multiple entities, including race, ethnicity, gender, gender identity, sexuality, disability, age, and citizenship, that reciprocally construct power relations and social inequalities.[34] As a result, aspects of intersectionality have been expounded upon in various fields of study. Edward Said introduced the traveling theory, which explains how a theory can evolve from its original stance. The theory suggests that the journey can cause a theory to be changed positively or negatively.[38] This theory helps us understand why intersectionality has been researched in women's studies, gender studies, cultural studies, media studies, and other interdisciplinary fields. The original intent surrounding intersectionality theory has been altered many times, but it has also benefited from multiple offshoots. Intersectionality has opened the door to the discovery of our own intersectional identities.

Although intersectionality and intersectional identities are often confounded, they are quite different. Intersectionality focuses on the intersection of identities that contribute to oppressive practices. The concept of intersecting identities is based on how certain aspects of our identity influence other identities. As I thought back to when understanding intersectional identities was most effective as a tool,

---

36. Bilge, "Intersectionality Undone: Saving Intersectionality from Feminist Intersectionality Studies."

37. Collins, "Intersectionality's Definitional Dilemmas

38. Said, "Traveling Theory (1982)."

I was reminded of an activity I did with one of my teams several years ago. I invited an external team to help work through our team's culture. The facilitator started us off with a relatively simple task. We were given a sheet of paper, and on the paper was a list of thirty or so identifiers. We were asked to circle each one that applied to our identity. For example, one field asked if you were a parent, the other asked if you spoke multiple languages, and another asked whether you were married or single. In full transparency, I've provided my responses to the activity below:

> *I am a man.*
>
> *I am heterosexual.*
>
> *I am African American.*
>
> *I am a first-generation American.*
>
> *My ethnic country of origin is the Democratic Republic of Congo.*
>
> *I am a proud father, husband, son, and brother.*
>
> *I am a millennial (just barely making the cut).*
>
> *I am an introvert.*
>
> *I have traveled to and lived in over thirty countries.*
>
> *I speak English and French.*
>
> *I am not affiliated with any political party.*
>
> *I'm Christian, nondenominational.*

Afterward, we totaled the number of fields we circled and shared with the group. Some people found that they had over twenty identities! Those who were comfortable shared some of their unique identities. I share this tool because it was an eye-opening experience hearing team members reveal parts of who they were that I never knew before, details they likely never felt comfortable sharing before the activity. It was also interesting to see the common intersections across our identities. such as race and social class or gender and access. We found many similarities among the team members; the experience helped the group develop an inclusive culture. We walked away understanding how we were all unique in our own ways; the exercise was a brilliant way to bring about those differences. It encouraged conversations we traditionally felt uncomfortable engaging in, fearing unintended, sometimes awkward discussions. In this day and age, understanding one's intersectional identities is crucial in the quest toward self-awareness. The philosopher Thales postulated, "The most difficult thing in life is to know yourself." The process of uncovering how multilayered we are as human beings can result in a lifelong journey. As the world becomes increasingly globalized, cultural identities will become even more apparent. As such, the GIL framework's first pillar centers on the cultural study of intersections.

Culture-Based Intersectional Identities

Before defining cultural and intersectional identities, there is a need to highlight the meaning behind the word "culture." Culture is the learned beliefs, values, rules, norms, symbols, and traditions common to a group of people.[39] Much like intersectionality, culture has been a focal point of research over the last thirty years. The research has led to a collection of dimensions of culture. The dimensions of culture were originally developed by social psychologist Geert Hofstede, who used the dimension to determine how cultures varied across the globe. In the end, his research defined six categories that contribute to culture, including power distance, individualism vs. collectivism, uncertainty

---

39 Northouse, *Leadership: Theory and Practice*, 434.

avoidance, gender egalitarianism, short-term vs. long-term orientation, and indulgence vs. restraint. Below are the definitions for each
dimension:

- *Power distance* refers to the degree to which members of a
group agree and expect power to be distributed unequally.
Power distance puts people into categories based on power.
Categories include authority, prestige, status, wealth, and
material possessions. Cultures that endorse low power distance
tend to be more egalitarian and regard others as equals
regardless of formal roles. Cultures that endorse high power
distance are more autocratic and hierarchical. Therefore, in
these cultures, followers respect power based on formal roles
and responsibilities.

- *Individualism vs. collectivism* refers to the degree to which
members of a group are integrated into that group. Cultures
that endorse individualist practices emphasize individuals'
rights, freedoms, and achievements. These cultures are
prone to members speaking up for themselves, whereas,
in collectivist cultures, members act as part of a collective
group. Collectivist members are loyal and faithful to the
group.

- *Uncertainty avoidance* refers to the degree to which members
depend on social norms, rituals, and procedures to avoid
uncertainty. Uncertainty avoidance is concerned with how
rules and laws make things predictable and thus reducing the
group's angst. Cultures with high uncertainty avoidance are
entrepreneurial-minded, with individuals likely to take more
risks. In cultures with low uncertainty avoidance, members
are less likely to take risks and make bold decisions. In such
cultures, business deals require longer to manifest and build
trust.

- *Femininity vs. masculinity* (gender egalitarianism) refers to the
degree to which members minimize gender role differences

and promote gender equality. In feministic cultures, values are placed in the ability to nurture and quality of life. The masculine cultures value competition, wealth building, and material possessions.

- *Short-term vs. long-term orientation* refers to the degree to which people engage in forward-looking behaviors such as planning and investing in the future. Long-term-oriented cultures place more importance on the future. They delay short-term gratification and focus on long-term growth. Short-term-oriented cultures focus on short-term success and gratification. They value quick results, respect for tradition, and fulfilling social obligations.

- *Indulgence vs. restraint* refers to the degree to which members control their impulses and desires. Indulgent cultures tend to enjoy life and have more fun compared to restrained cultures. Restrained cultures control their need for gratification through social norms.

Cultural dimensions are undeniably woven into our identities; however, it more broadly defines central tendencies within a group. For example, in the United States—the land with the most complex set of cultural identities—Hofstede Insights found power distance to be low, whereas individualism is high.[40] The US is known as the land of liberty and justice for all, even though many disenfranchised citizens may not subscribe to the notion that freedom is equally nor equitably distributed. Therefore, using the dimension to help

---

40. Hofstede Insights, "United States - Hofstede Insights."

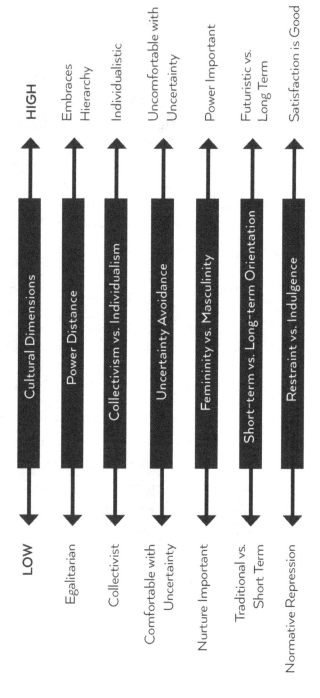

Figure 3.1. Culture Dimensions[41]

distinguish cultures along the spectrum is much more appropriate, not solely along the two endpoints. As seen in figure 3.1, culture dimensions are all displayed on a spectrum from low to high.

Cultural-based intersections recognize the points at which a cultural identity or identities converge in each person's life. Racism, sexism, imperialism, class exploitation, and language discrimination are created from culture-based oppression. Cultural identities can disadvantage and disempower a group. Therefore, recognizing how cultural identities promote oppressive behavior is critical to any organization. Let's explore instances of cultural-based intersections:

1. In the United States, the Asian Immigrant Women Advocates (AIWA) has used its organization to show how gender, immigration status, and poverty are employed to exacerbate labor exploitation, how language is used to confine limited English-speaking women to jobs below their skill levels, and how gender hierarchies at work and in the home hinder the development of women as leaders.[42] The group realized the need for gender egalitarianism. However, it had to be coupled with aspects of other dimensions, including a low power distance and a short-term orientation.

2. The Nicaragua solidarity movement was created to bring aware-ness to the oppression in Latin American countries, specifically in Nicaragua. The country had been invaded and occupied

41 Adapted from Corporate Finance Institute, "Hofstede's Cultural Dimensions Theory."

42. Chun, Lipsitz, and Shin, "Intersectionality as a Social Movement Strategy: Asian Immigrant Women Advocates.

by the US in the 1930s. Therefore, the movement drew US citizens' attention to the suffering resulting from US policy toward Nicaragua and promoted a sustained social movement by US citizens against their government's Nicaraguan policy.[43] The US authority displayed power distance toward Nicaraguan leadership contributed significantly to the oppressive actions.[44]

3. Researchers have found a disproportionate representation of minority children in child welfare systems documented in many areas worldwide. Identities such as race, ethnicity, culture, gender, or socioeconomic status can influence child maltreatment. Three principles explain cultural intersectionality in the context of child maltreatment. First, social and cultural groups are heterogeneous. Second, power differentials are frequently neglected but central to social structure. Third, individuals may identify with more than one social group. The cultural dimensions of power distance and collectivism are in effect.[45]

One of the central elements of Crenshaw's research reveals intersectionality as a coalition of identities that seek not to divide but rather to create avenues for learning. Crenshaw explained, "My focus on the intersections of race and gender only highlights the need to account for multiple grounds of identity when considering how the social world is constructed."[46] Similarly, the three case studies reveal intersectional identities from different cultural vantage points.

43. Perla, "Heirs of Sandino."

44. Carastathis, "Intersectionality: Origins, Contestations, Horizons."

45. Stewart and McDermott, "Gender in Psychology."

46. Crenshaw, "Mapping the Margins: Intersectionality, Identity Politics, and Violence against Women of Color, 1245.

Having someone who can interpret which cultural dimension is at play when a situation of oppression is present can help accelerate the path to resolution. I define this role as a *cultural intersectionalist*. The cultural intersectionalist defines the culturally relevant dimension as it relates to the cultural identity or identities that intersect, considering oppressive forces at play.

The Global Inclusive Leadership Imperative

I found that the opposite of inclusion is not only exclusion; it's oppression. Therefore, to build an inclusive environment, leaders must seek to eliminate any semblance of oppressive forces. Intersectionality and intersectional identities as a tool, a theory, and a field of study can support the path toward global inclusivity. As mentioned, intersectionality theory is multifaceted and can be used in a variety of ways. In their article entitled, "Intersectionality as a Social Movement Strategy: Asian Immigrant Women Advocates," researchers Jennifer Chun, George Lipsitz, and Young Shin explain how intersectionality as an analytical tool ". . . can be used strategically to take inventory of differences, to identify potential contradictions and conflicts, and to recognize the split and conflicting identities not as obstacles to solidarity but as valuable evidence about problems unsolved and as new coalitions that need to be formed. Group identities are vital for collective mobilizations for rights, resources, and recognition."[39]

The intersectional identities activity I shared earlier sparked enough interest in me, and it caused me to explore more practices for developing teams and driving and sustaining inclusionary efforts. This same curiosity developed in me at a young age in Dakar. Not everyone will have the opportunity to be exposed to culture through travel. Nevertheless, the opportunity to learn is afforded to everyone. Leadership is dependent on competencies, one of which is the ability to learn. Phycologists Nancy Adler and Susan Bartholomew suggest that global leaders possess the following five cross-cultural competencies associated with learning:[47]

- Leaders should understand the business, political, and cultural environment.

- Leaders should comprehend tastes, trends, and technologies in other cultures.

- Leaders should be able to work simultaneously with people from other cultures.

- Leaders should be comfortable with living and/or communicating with other cultures.

- Leaders should be able to relate with people from other cultures and do so not from a position of superiority but rather from a place of equality.

I believe these are great starting points. For leadership to sustain inclusive aspirations, the questions leaders ask themselves must be deep enough to invoke radical change. Here are a few questions leaders should ask to ensure oppressive behaviors are eradicated:

- Which of your identities or attitudes are defined by privilege in a dominant culture, and which are potentially marginalized or oppressed?

---

47. Adler and Bartholomew, "Managing Globally Competent People.""

- Who in your circle can verify the first question?

- How can you ensure team members feel safe having conversations about intersectional and cultural identity issues?

- Where can intersectionality as a tool for learning be applied in your organizations?

Next, let's explore how global inclusive leaders tie culture into their strategy.

CHAPTER 4.

Culture is Strategy

Our time was nearing its end in Senegal. Since the war in Liberia persisted, my parents decided that we would relocate temporarily to the Democratic Republic of Congo (DRC). They shared so many stories of family members we would meet as we entered our country of origin for the first time. My siblings and I were eager to meet our extended family members. At that time, we had only seen them through pictures. We finally had an opportunity to meet face-to-face.

From the minute we landed, I was overwhelmed by the many family members who came to the airport to welcome us. I remember thinking maybe they had confused us with some celebrities. It almost seemed as if everyone had their eyes on us, and it felt great. We left the airport and arrived at this property surrounded by a concrete enclosure. None of the neighbors had fences, amplifying the fact that this house was different. When we pulled in the ten-foot-high pure metal gates, we were enamored by the equally impressive grandeur of the house. It was enormous; it was also abnormally different from the neighboring homes. When we walked through the front door, a huge feast had been prepared for the family, with even more friends and family members waiting to share a greeting. Yes, it was a bit engulfing, but it was the right place for a kid who sought this type of community.

Eventually, the honeymoon phase was over, and we were enrolled in public school. When we first arrived in Liberia, my siblings and I were enrolled in a local public school. For kids who had previously spent their youth in the US school system, this school was a drastic change. Most notably, we experienced for the first time a school population made up of predominantly native Black people. While we had the same skin tone, we always stood out like sore thumbs. We eventually transferred to an international school that offered more cultural diversity, which proved to be a much easier transition to our newfound life. Now, in DRC, we were faced with a similar situation.

We attended École Malula, a combined primary and secondary school about twenty minutes from our home. I remember how atypical the school was compared to what I had seen in the past. It was rather large, with a population of over a thousand students. The campus seemed to stretch for miles, with classrooms set up like staggered row houses. On the first day, walking through the outdoor hall was daunting. Growing up, I never enjoyed the first day of school, but that day was particularly troubling. I remember holding back tears as I walked into the dark, dingy room. Nevertheless, tears started running down my face as soon as the teacher pointed me to my seat.

I would eventually acclimate to the environment, but certain things would remain peculiar. For one, the official language in the school was French; however, most students spoke Lingala in and after class. We started learning French after school in Liberia, but I was still a novice. Lingala was utterly foreign. Another thing, uniforms were mandatory. The traditional style included a white polo shirt with navy pants for boys and a white collared shirt with a navy skirt for girls. The length of hair had to be no longer than a centimeter long for boys and girls. My mother was not willing to accept this rule for my elder sister. My sister, who loved her lengthy hair, was also not the least bit thrilled. After several reminders were sent home, my mom would finally set up a meeting with the school leaders and let them know that her daughter's hair would not be touched, and that was the end of that matter. There wasn't any debate. My parents were looked at differently; they were part of a privileged group that had traveled abroad and now reaped the benefits of their experience. Yes, they were Congolese, but they had made it out; they were part of the diaspora that returned home.

We would immediately be reminded that we were different; we were the "American kids." Not only were we the American kids, but surprisingly the rules didn't apply to us; we were favored and held to a higher esteem. Some kids were envious, others were visibly resentful, and some grew increasingly interested, a storyline with which I was familiar. On one occasion, I recall my teacher coming to my house in the afternoon. I was shocked; I had never seen or heard of a teacher coming to a student's home. *Why did he come? How did he know where I lived?* The questions kept running through my mind. I would learn later that he came to ask for money. Most teachers were grossly underpaid and had to look for alternate ways to make ends meet. Showing up uninvited was a bold move, but it paid off as my mother gave him enough funds to send him home satisfied.

My experiences overseas proved to me how cultures vary greatly. We've touched on culture from the intersectionality perspective. This chapter will highlight culture from a strategic perspective. Although often put at odds, strategy and culture are mutually beneficial. Culture cannot exist without a strategy, and strategy cannot exist without culture.

Culture and Organizations

Strategy is an essential component of effective leadership and accomplishing an organization's goals. It involves collectively agreeing on priorities. Organizations create strategic plans to implement those priorities to accomplish their purpose and goals.[48] Over the years, organizations have applied strategies to sustain their growth plans. Organizational development is the process organizations implement to help build change and achieve greater effectiveness. It is inherently a Western ideology. Organizational development's underlying assumptions and methods are highly influenced by industrialized cultures.[49] Therefore, it is plausible for approaches to be developed that contradict the values of a foreign culture. For organizations to create inclusive working environments, they must start by understanding how to apply culture to their strategy.

Culture can be observed from two angles, organizational and local. Organizational culture tends to be dominant and relatively independent from the local culture.[50] Working overseas, I witnessed the two cultures battle often. I worked for a global organization that asked many of its employees to achieve a specific target, often requiring late nights. The concept worked well in the US; however, when leadership decided to move some of the operations to Europe, resistance from the local culture was evident. The local culture emphasized family life and relaxation; working late hours did not align with the organization's culture. Organizational culture must not

---

48. Ackermann and Eden, Making Strategy: Mapping Out Strategic Success.

49. Cummings and Worley, Organization Development and Change.

50. Lundby and Jolton, Going Global: *Practical Applications and Recommendations for HR and OD Professionals in the Global Workplace.*

only align with strategy but also with the local culture. To uncover this cultural complexity, let us first define culture in the context of the organization and society.

As mentioned in the previous chapter, culture is the learned beliefs, values, rules, norms, symbols, and traditions common to a group of people.[51] From an organizational standpoint, culture is defined as the accumulated shared learning of a group as it solves its problems of external adaption and internal integration. As seen in figure 4.1, this shared learning can be divided into three levels: behaviors and artifacts, beliefs and values, and basic assumptions.

1. Behaviors and artifacts are the visible and evident aspects of the group. Examples of artifacts in local culture include architecture, language, clothing, manners of address, emotional displays, myths, and stories. When I observed the various languages in school, that was my way of learning the culture. I learned how to address others and how a slight tone adjustment could change a word's meaning. When the kids said "Nakobeta yo"—"I'm going to hit you"—on the school ground, it meant something very different from when my grandmother said the same thing. She meant it as a pleasantry, at least that is what I was led to believe. In an organization, artifacts can include but are not limited to technology, service, product, innovation, and style. Observed behaviors are also artifacts represented by routines or rituals; however, these behaviors are hard to decipher. Local observed behaviors include religious practices or archaeological structures such as pyramids or ruins. Although easily observed, it may require time to truly uncover the meaning. Observed behavior's organizational culture can include organization charts, charters, or internal process documents.

---

51 Northouse, *Leadership: Theory and Practice,* 434

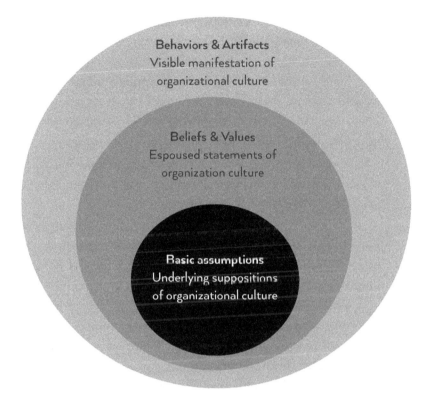

Figure 4.1. Levels of Culture [52]

These elements can reveal a lot about the organization; however, the meaning becomes increasingly evident when you work within the organization for some time.

2. *Beliefs and values* are what we believe to be true and the guiding principles and assumptions that tell us what is wrong and right. Psychologist Edgar Schein asserted that beliefs and values must be empirically tested and support group problems to be considered underlying assumptions.[53] However, certain values, especially those with moral implications, cannot be

---

52. Adapted from Northouse, *Leadership: Theory and Practice*

53. Hatch and Schultz, *Organizational Identity: A Reader.*

tested. In such cases, social validation helps create consensus. I may have found it strange for my teacher to come to my house and ask for money; however, in the Congo, as in many developing countries, asking for money is quite common. My mother recounts that it's become so ingrained in the culture that some children grow up knowing how to ask for money as a skill. Such behavior takes on a negative connotation in Western cultures. Organizationally, underlying assumptions[53] from which beliefs and values originate must be congruent with principles that guide performance.

3. *Basic assumptions* are unconscious thoughts, beliefs, perceptions, and feelings.[54] A collection of assumptions will ultimately develop a mental memory. When you associate with others who have the same assumptions, the assumption becomes perpetuated into reality. Basic assumptions create a sense of identity amongst members who share the same values.[55] Our basic assumptions can be unconscious. In my work with the global organization, the US employees assumed that everyone would be comfortable working late to accomplish the goals. Our European counterparts found our willingness to stay beyond traditional working hours incomprehensible. As such, basic assumptions may not change behavior, but they can help explain its roots.

This three-level model of culture facilitates understanding of the cultural phenomenon. The model can be applied in the context of local or organizational culture. Let's explore how culture intercepts with strategy.

---

53. Schein, *Organizational Culture and Leadership.*

54. Schein, *Organizational Culture and Leadership (Jossey-Bass business & management series).*

55. Hatch and Schultz, *Organizational Identity: A Reader.*

The Importance of the Local Cultural Perspective and Strategy

Culture has been and will always be linked to the study of organizations. Culture is the foundation of the organization, which forms culture through vision, purpose, and goals. At the same time, organizations are part of a larger external culture that has implications for the internal culture. Many well-documented business cases explain the challenges organizations have had expanding overseas while attempting to maintain the same corporate culture. Walmart, for example, had tried for nearly ten years to grow in the German market. The world's largest retailer found several challenges, the main one being culture. German customers complained about the hearty greetings from staff and packers at every checkout. A greeting is an aspect of the customer experience that has worked well in the US; however, German buyers did not embrace the method. In the US, a smile is a standard welcome, whereas a smile can be somewhat disingenuous and unnerving in Germany.

The notion that any customer group would resonate with Walmart's "Everyday Low Price" model encouraged the company to expand globally. Walmart's research showed that the German consumer was open to cost-conscious options. Furthermore, the centrally located country could serve as a hub to expand into other parts of Europe. The supplier network and distribution capabilities proved to be solid indicators for success in the market.[56] However, the high labor costs, labor unions, and other factors also impacted Walmart's less than stellar business environment.

Many scholars have argued that Walmart's eventual exit from

---

56. Kaelberer, "Wal-Mart Goes to Germany: Culture, Institutions, and the Limits of Globalization."

the German market was driven by its inability to adjust to the host culture.[52] Other retailers, most notably Ikea, Amazon, and eBay, have been successful in the German market. Walmart was still relatively new to global expansion and thus had not considered the need for decentralization.[57] At the time, the company had brought a US-centric model with US leaders to a foreign land. However, the policies, marketing initiatives, and in-store capabilities needed to align with the needs of the local culture. Incorporating local leaders into the decision-making process helps to shape an understanding of needs in the local market. Centralization and decentralization stand on opposite sides of the power spectrum. Decentralization allows for a balance of power. However, it is less about shifting power; it's instead about ensuring the concentration of power does not solely reside at the top. Decentralization allows for autonomy; it opens the door to addressing local needs. Deciding whether to keep the power centralized versus decentralized is a function of organizational development.

Hofstede's research on national cultures can be tied to organizational development, including power distance, uncertainty avoidance, individualism, context orientation, and achievement orientation. Table 4.1 provides a list of the cultural values (dimensions) with examples of the organizational custom when the value is at one extreme.

Understanding how culture impacts organizational customs can help determine the need for change or strategy design efforts. It can also determine how quickly a change effort will take place, who will be involved in the change process, and whether decisions will be made by a member in authority or by consensus amongst team members. In

57. Grose, "Wal-Mart's Rollback: After Retreating from Germany, the Giant Retailer Makes a Last Stand in Britain."

VALUE	DEFINITION	ORGANIZATION CUSTOMS WHEN VALUE IS AT ONE EXTREME
Power Distance	The extent to which members of a society accept that power is distributed unequally in an organization	→ Decision-making is autocratic → Employees are not likely to disagree → Privilege is given to influential people
Uncertainty Avoidance	The extent to which members of an organization tolerate the unfamiliar and unpredictable	→ Clear roles are preferred → Conflict is undesired → Change comes with resistance
Individualism	Extend to which members believe they should be responsible for themselves and their immediate families	→ Personal initiative is encouraged → Members value time → Competition is accepted
Context Orientation	The extent to which words carry the meaning of a message	→ Ceremony and routines are common → Structure is less formal, fewer written policies
Achievement Orientation	The extent to which members value assertiveness and the acquisition of material goods	→ Achievement is reflected in wealth and recognition → Decisiveness is valued → Gender roles are clearly differentiated

Table 4.1. Cultural Values and Organization Customs [58]

some situations, organizational development can perfectly align with the local culture; however, less developed economies may require an assessment to determine the ideal cultural identity. Every organization

58. Adapted from Cummings and Worley, *Organization Development and Change.*"

must evaluate the need for local responsiveness and global integration. Local responsiveness is the extent to which business goals are dependent on customized products, services, support, packaging, or any other aspects specific to the local culture, whereas global integrations are the extent to which business goals require tight coordination with people, plant and equipment, products, and services worldwide.[59]

Whether the organization is international, global, multinational, or transnational, organizational development methods can be put into practice for cultural change and strategic initiatives. Table 4.2 describes the characteristics of these methods. Not all intervention methods are appropriate, which is why it's critical to determine the organizational strategy and structure that create an environment for cultural initiatives to thrive. Cross-cultural training, role descriptions, and cultural development all contribute to attaining strategic change.

The Global Inclusive Leadership Imperative

Organizations can use organizational development to operate at home and in host cultures. To do so, the organizational strategy must fit with the cultural needs. Global inclusive leaders are attentive to building organizational structures that support strategic needs in line with the cultural environment. My time in the DRC taught me a vital lesson on knowing and scanning the environment and observing key cultural differences or similarities. I used this information to help me adapt and sometimes conform to my surroundings. From an organizational standpoint, leaders require the ability to assess the cultural landscape to determine the potential changes needed for

---

59. Cummings and Worley, *Organization Development and Change.*

TYPE OF ORGANIZATION	STRATEGY	STRUCTURE	CULTURE AND ORGANIZATION DESIGN METHODS
International	Goal to increase foreign revenue	Centralized international division	→ Cross-cultural training → Strategic planning
Global	Goal to increase efficiency through volume	Centralized, balanced, and coordinated activities	→ Role clarification → Senior management team building
Multinational	Goal to increase local responsiveness through specialization	Decentralized operations, centralized planning	→ Local management team building → Reward system → Strategic alliances
Transnational	Goal to increase learning and responsiveness through integration	Decentralized, worldwide coordination	→ Cultural development → Rotation programs → Building aligned vision

Table 4.2. Cultural and Organizational Design Methods [54]

operational success. Here are a few questions leaders should ask to align strategy with culture:

- How should organizational development be conducted in light of the local culture?

- Will the organizational development initiatives contribute to people-specific improvements?

- Will our organizational development initiatives help preserve the local cultural values?

- Who will need to be at the table to ensure these local cultural values are preserved?

Our next chapter will shift from strategy to morality as we consider personal values, organizational values, and ethics.

Moral Capabilities

CHAPTER 5.

The Psychology of a Leader

Living in the Democratic Republic of Congo was the best of times and the worst of times. On the one hand, I loved being surrounded by family. I lived a relatively simple life. I went to school, spent time with family, and played outdoor games. On the other hand, I lived in a country on the brink of war. The Congo was going through a democratic transition marked by periodic civil unrest. Like the situation we had escaped from in Liberia, the DRC, named Zaire at the time, was plagued by several longstanding issues. Some of those issues included ethnic intolerance, the illegal exploitation of the country's vast natural resources, and a Congolese elite that benefited from the chaos.[60] The news coverage seemed to report disputes that mainly impacted other parts of the country, but one day, we would feel the impact right in our vicinity.

One warm summer afternoon, my siblings and I were in school. There had been rumors of the approaching rebel forces entering the city limits of Kinshasa. Outside of the students and teachers being on high alert, the day seemed like any other day. No one knew what

---

60. Maina and Gacheche, "Conflict in the DRC: 5 Articles That Explain What's Gone Wrong."

to expect, so a business-as-usual mentality only made sense. Out of nowhere, I saw my uncle appear at my classroom door; he came to pull me out of class. Without much explanation, he rushed my siblings and me off the school grounds. The further we got from my classroom, the more I noticed many other students making their way to the exit. By the time we reached the school gates, hundreds of students were vigorously fleeing from the school grounds. As we jumped into our vehicle, there was commotion everywhere. Once on the road, it looked as if we were driving in the wrong way as seemingly thousands of citizens sprinted past us in the opposite direction; but we had no choice; we had to take this route home. I kept wondering what was happening and what was waiting for us ahead.

Minutes later, we barely reached the edge of our neighborhood before the rebels (insurgents from the military) approached, heavily armed. I remember, about half a mile ahead of us, seeing armed men marching toward us, shooting several rounds of ammunition as we took a sharp turn into our neighborhood, avoiding stray bullets. This chilling visual is one I have plastered in my memory bank to this day. Once we arrived home, family members immediately boarded up windows with extra zinc roof panels used to seal the roof. The rest of the family sought refuge in the middle of the house, where bullets were less likely to penetrate. At the time, I felt like we were in the middle of a movie scene, experiencing a thrilling scene firsthand. We had no idea what was coming next, but we braced for the worst. My abnormal excitement would soon turn to anxiety as we waited for a sign that things had returned to some semblance of normal. By nightfall, we received word that the streets were clear.

With the little French I knew and the context clues I gathered, I could determine what family members were discussing. The mood was somber, but that didn't stop what appeared to be a lively discussion. The frustration was evident, but no one was willing to cast blame. It was clear this was not the first time such events had occurred in the city or the country, for that matter. At the time, I was outraged that any group would be willing to go to such lengths to disrupt our peace. In the aftermath, I learned more about what was behind these moments of unrest. The DRC had always been a notorious hot spot for conflict. Since its independence from Belgium on June 30, 1960, Congo has experienced several geopolitical bouts. By January of 1961, the prime minister, Patrice Lumumba, was assassinated by Congolese rivals. Several assassination attempts had been undertaken as Lumumba was seen as a threat to US interest in the Congo. His death highlights the involvement of different actors in Congolese affairs, most notably the US and Belgium.

Interest in the DRC originated long before its independence. In 1884, the Berlin conference would, in large part, open the door to the Scramble for Africa, the colonization of a majority of African nations by European nations.[61] Only seven months before the Berlin Congress partitioned Africa to Western countries, the US was the first country in the world to recognize the Congo as a Belgian territory. The DRC is a land with an abundance of raw materials, including copper, cobalt, gold, diamonds, coltan, zinc, tin, and tungsten, to name a few. When Portuguese traders arrived from Europe in the 1480s, they realized they had stumbled upon a land of vast natural wealth, not to mention the human capital that would eventually become essential to the slave-trade movement. The Portuguese realized that they would need to create instability to take control of the supply of goods. They sought to destroy indigenous political

---

61 Wack, *The Story of the Congo Free State: Social, Political, and Economic Aspects of the Belgian System of Government in Central Africa.*

forces and provide rebel forces with money and weapons to create division.[62]

With this context, Mobutu Sese Seko emerged as the Zairian president after independence. The US and Belgium saw him as a lesser threat compared to Lumumba's Pan-African approach, given Mobutu's willingness to favor pro-Western styles. A US-backed prime minister, Cyrille Adoula, would eventually take over Lumumba's role.[63] Mobutu's government ruled the nation from 1965 to 1997. His leadership accounted for most of the country's downfall. Mobutu was the quintessential pseudo-transformational leader. Yes, he had charisma and knew how to get people to follow him. But he exploited the country for its riches, leading to increased national debt and inflation. He reportedly had a villa in Switzerland worth $2.5 million and an estimated $4 billion in bank assets.[64] He promoted foreign and domestic policies that allowed for corruption under his reign. He was cited for several human rights violations throughout his tenure. With the support of Western allies, Mobutu was widely regarded as having systematically looted the country for thirty years.

It baffled me how a person who had seen his country's suffering before and after its independence could turn to rule with such negligence. Under his rule, a war would break out in the country that would eventually be known as Africa's first world war. The war claimed up to six million lives, either as a direct result of fighting

---

62 BBC News, "DR Congo: Cursed by Its Natural Wealth."

63. "Foreign Relations of the United States, 1964–1968, Volume XXIII, Congo, 1960–1968 - Office of the Historian."

64 Transparency International, "Seize Mobutu's Wealth or Lose Your Own Money, Western Governments Told - Press."

or secondary impacts such as disease and malnutrition.[65] Mobutu's leadership is emblematic of leaders who choose to satisfy their own self-indulgence and harmful intentions. He was not alone; many actors in Europe and the US carried the same indulgent nature.

What drives leaders to act in such cruel and egotistical ways? I wonder if we could look at how we make decisions to determine leaders' tendencies or intuition. The study of the moral psychology of leaders helps to undercover how personality and characteristics impact leadership. Psychological factors support a leader's capacity to demonstrate emotional or cultural intelligence. It also reveals how leaders treat followers. The following chapters will explore how global inclusive leaders can use their moral competencies to avoid blind spots. Let's introduce psychological factors into global inclusive leadership.

The Evil Side of Leadership

Before we examine the psychology of moral leaders, let's analyze the leader at the opposite end of the spectrum—the destructive leader. Mobutu's corrupt behavior is emblematic of this type of unethical leader. His actions were self-serving, and he knowingly and maliciously took advantage of his people. Bernard Bass, scholar and author of the book *Transformational Leadership,* coined the term "pseudo-transformational leadership" to define such leaders. Leaders who act

65. Reyntjens, "The Great African War: Congo and Regional Geopolitics, 1996-2006.

66 Bass, "From Transactional to Transformational Leadership: Learning to Share the Vision."

in their self-interest often fall under this leadership style. Under the influence of such a leader, followers are often misdirected away from their own best interests and those of the organization.[66] This type of leader is manipulative and discourages independent thought in followers. Most people would agree that Adolf Hitler, Joseph Stalin, or Saddam Hussein fit into this description as historically atrocious and dysfunctional leaders.

Destructive leadership behavior is the systematic and repeated behavior by a leader, supervisor, or manager that violates the legitimate interest of the organization by undermining and sabotaging the organization's goals, tasks, resources, or effectiveness and decreases motivation or job satisfaction in their subordinates.[67] Destructive leadership comprises three distinct attributes: the destructive leader, the susceptible follower, and the conducive environment. The *destructive leader* is the type who uses power and coercion for personal gain. The *susceptible follower* is either a conformer who goes along with the leader to satisfy unmet needs or the colluder who goes along with the leader because they identify with the leader's beliefs or are driven by their selfish ambitions. Lastly, a *conducive environment* is one where instability is evident and where leaders have the power to make radical changes as they see fit.[68] The visual, figure 5.1, illustrates how the destructive leader can thrive in this toxic triangle.

In her book, *The Allure of Toxic Leaders*, Jean Lipman-Blumen identified six factors that foster destructive leadership:[70]

---

67 Einarsen, Aasland, and Skogstad, "Destructive Leadership Behaviour: A Definition and Conceptual Model, 207."

68 Padilla, Hogan, and Kaiser, "The Toxic Triangle: Destructive Leaders, Susceptible Followers, and Conducive Environments."

Figure 5.1. The Toxic Triangle[69]

1. Our need for reassuring authority figures—the need for leaders to provide guidance, similar to how a parent provides guidance to a child.

2. Our need for security and certainty—the desire to keep a balance in our beliefs and attitudes, as an undocumented worker may behave toward a threatening employer.

3. Our need to feel chosen or special—the need to believe you are on the right side and others are not, as a white supremacist would feel over other races.

---

69 Lipman-Blumen, The Allure of Toxic Leaders: Why We Follow Destructive Bosses and Corrupt Politicians--and How We Can Survive Them

70. Adapted from Padilla, Hogan, and Kaiser, "The Toxic Triangle: Destructive Leaders, Susceptible Followers, and Conducive Environments", 180.

4. Our need for membership in the human community—the need to feel accepted by a group, similar to how a pledgee might feel once accepted in a fraternity.

5. Our fear of ostracism, isolation, and social death—the need to feel included and not disliked, as one might feel when part of a destructive group.

6. Our fear of powerlessness to challenge a bad leader—the need to conform to the group's norms, as one might do to avoid confrontation.

Destructive leaders prevent inclusionary practices and create psychological barriers to organizational success. The Global Inclusive Leadership Framework highlights the need for leaders to build awareness of intersectional identities as an initial phase. The second phase shifts the focus from the "me" to the "us"—from the leader to the followers. The "us" considers how leaders and followers operate as part of a social group. Leaders do not function in a vacuum; they exist in a position of influence on others. As such, the leader's behavior or leadership style comes into question when moral and ethical dilemmas are in play.

Uncovering Ethical Behavior

Ethical issues are a core concern in most organizational and societal settings, given the many corporate and political scandals of the twenty-first century. Leaders have always been at the center of the issue. Even in the presence of documentation, including pages of policies, codes of ethics, codes of conduct, organizational values, and company cultures, unethical issues persist in organizations every day. These issues typically result from inappropriate leadership behavior, such as embezzlement, insider stock trading, expense account fraud, sexual harassment, and involvement in conflicts of interest. For example, in 2010, Mark Hurd, Hewlett Packard's CEO, was relieved of his duties after the board determined that he had engaged in inappropriate behavior that violated HP's standard of business conduct.[71] Nearly ten years later, Steve Easterbrook, McDonald's CEO, was ousted after admitting to a consensual relationship with an employee. Even with McDonald's formal policy restricting certain consensual relationships, Easterbrook violated the policy nonetheless.[72]

The most well-known of all unethical leaders came by way of Bernie Madoff. In late 2008, Madoff was arrested on one count of securities fraud for allegedly operating a multibillion-dollar Ponzi scheme from his investment advisory business. By the following year, Madoff was sentenced to 150 years in prison. In an interview from prison, Madoff told the *New York Times* that he felt that some banks and hedge funds "had to know." One can surmise that people around Madoff did know about his unethical behavior but chose to look the other way; others may have advised him down the wrong path to further their self-interest. Regardless, Madoff's unethical practices resulted in several negative consequences for all stakeholders. Authors Max Bazerman and Ovul Sezer explain two psychological processes that clarify how others may not have noticed Madoff's actions. First, their awareness of the developing problem was

---

71 O'Brien, "Mark Hurd's Leadership Failure."

72 Heathfield, "Avoiding Ethical Lapses in the Workplace."

73. Bazerman and Sezer, "Bounded Awareness: Implications for Ethical Decision Making."

bounded or limited. Second, they also engaged in unethical action without intending to do anything wrong and without knowing they were doing so. With this in mind, they offered two reasons for the failures:[73]

1. *Bounded rationality* is central to organizational behavior. Bounded rationality argues that "human rationality is very limited, very much bounded by the situation and human computational powers."[74] Leaders can be "bounded" by factors such as time, emotions, or environment. As such, under the decision-making process, individuals tend to make suboptimal choices instead of spending the necessary time to research and analyze the situation. We all fall victim to bounded rationality. Consider this situation as an example. A retail shop is facing financial challenges. To make up for the deficit, they have the option to let go of some employees, invest in marketing initiatives to help encourage sales, or cut prices on available inventory. To appease the immediate concerns of leaders at the headquarters, the district manager decides to let go of a few employees. The action produces immediate financial results; however, in the long run, the challenges might return. The leader's actions were ineffective because of the failure to assess all options and react quickly due to time as a limitation.

2. *Focalism* is the tendency to focus too much on a particular event (the "focal event") and too little on other important events.[75] Also known as the focusing illusion, focalism shows how a leader might pay too much attention to a subset of available information while neglecting other vital details. For

---

74. Simon, Reason in *Human Affairs*, 34.

75. Gilbert and Wilson, "Miswanting: Some Problems in the Forecasting of Future Affective States."

example, when a reporter asked, "How is your organization performing?" a leader responded in the affirmative. However, if the reporter asked the question differently, "Given the declining sales over the last quarter, how is your organization performing?" now the focus has shifted. The leaders might be more prone to address the question in terms of the declining sales.

We are all, at times, blinded by our perceptions and biases that enable unethical actions. As a result, we all misjudge our ability to act ethically. Furthermore, we might not recognize our self-serving predispositions, thus the importance of understanding *bounded ethicality*. Bounded ethicality describes the systemic and predictable ways people make decisions without realizing the implications of their behavior. Bounded ethicality concerns those who make harmful decisions, especially when those decisions do not align with the decision maker's conscious beliefs and preferences.[76] *Bounded awareness* suggests that our perception and decision-making are constrained in ways we may not realize. There is, therefore, a gap between who we believe we are and who we truly are in these ethical situations. Every individual's "want self" must give voice to the "should self," but that is not always the case. Bounded awareness focuses on a cognitive failure, and bounded ethicality focuses on an ethical failure. The failure to notice and act on unethical issues around us constitutes an ethical failure.[77]

76. Bazerman and Tenbrunsel, *Blind Spots: Why We Fail to Do What's Right and What to Do about It.*

77. Bazerman and Sezer, "Bounded Awareness: Implications for Ethical Decision Making."

78. Northouse, *Leadership: Theory and Practice.*

The Global Inclusive Leadership Imperative

Leaders should display behaviors and make decisions that promote ethical business practices. Ethical leadership is concerned with leadership behavior, their choices, and how they respond to given circumstances.[78] The more a leader can influence followers, the more likely the organization can ultimately accomplish its goals. Therefore, evaluating a leader's ability to act ethically in any environment is essential. From a psychological standpoint, effective leaders should recognize the need for change and the need to become increasingly self-aware of unethical traps. Here are a few questions leaders should ask to create ethical environments:

- Where in the organization do we find threats of ethical challenges or blind spots?

- What ethical and potentially destructive behaviors am I exhibiting that contribute to my ability to lead?

- How can the organization prevent the creation of toxic environments?

- How can I help my teams understand the shared priority of safeguarding our ethical values?

When faced with ethical dilemmas, leaders should evaluate all options and select the most ethical one. Does it sound overly simple? It is. For instance, simply asking yourself what your mom would think of your decision may help you achieve a good outcome. Applying

---

79. *Xu, Loi, and Ngo, "Ethical Leadership Behavior and Employee Justice Perceptions: The Mediating Role of Trust in Organization."*

the "mom test" can assist with understanding that every situation has an ethical component.[72] Global inclusive leaders are moral agents for organizations.[79] What we consider good or bad may not resonate in a different culture. Let's examine how ethics apply in the global context.

CHAPTER 6.

Combating Ethical Paradoxes

The political situation in the DRC continued to worsen, and eventually, the decision was made to uproot the family once again. We spent less than a year in Kinshasa and were off to our next adventure. This time, we found our way back to West Africa's Atlantic coast, to Guinea-Bissau. Guinea-Bissau was a rather interesting country; when we arrived in 1990, it had only received its independence from colonial rule eighteen years prior. There was clearly a lot of development work to be done, and my dad was brought in to help provide technical support with UNDP. Finally, we appeared to find a country that was in peacetime. After short-lived experiences in Liberia, Senegal, and the DRC, we would call Guinea-Bissau home for the next three-plus years.

I grew to love Bissau, the capital city. It didn't have the cultural elements I appreciated in Liberia and Senegal or the family I had long-awaited in the DRC. Nevertheless, the country had an undeniable essence. It's one of the smallest and poorest countries globally, and from my perspective as a kid, I resonated with the simplicity of life there. The dirt roads, the kids playing in the towns, the street vendors, it somehow felt very familial. It's incredible how language barriers rarely impact children for too long. We could play games with neighbors without understanding a word. Portuguese, the country's official language, was not widely spoken by the locals. We didn't take time to learn the language either; we went to a French-speaking private school. Most of our friends were children of ambassadors, diplomats, or foreign businessmen and women, who all attended the same school.

We attended Victor Hugo School, a French extension program about ten minutes from our home. The total population of students could not have been more than eighty. The school provided both primary and secondary education in an unconventional fashion. We shared classrooms with students from different grade levels. I was in the same class as my elder sister for the first time. All assignments were mailed to France to be graded to ensure that we received the same level of education as a student would receive in the French system. We could only use a blue ballpoint ink pen to write our assignments, the type that requires refill cartridges, and we could only write in cursive. Failure to follow any rule would result in point deductions. I was not a fan of all the seemingly unnecessary regulations, but I enjoyed the friends I made, which made up for the grading requirements. I remember being sick one day, and when my mom told me I would have to stay home, I immediately started sobbing. That's how much I loved attending the school, a striking difference from the kid who had not previously enjoyed school.

Victor Hugo brought together a small community of expatriates. We knew the owners of the biggest retail shop in Bissau, a Lebanese family that lived a few blocks away. They had two children attending the school. I frequently spent time at the Italian ambassador's residence, whose son had a few of us over to play soccer, swim in his pool, or enjoy many other attractions on the estate. I was close friends with a kid named Carlos, whose dad worked with my dad at the United Nations. Carlos, like me, was born in the US, but his family originated in South America. We had an instant connection. However, my best friend was Gregory, a French kid from Marseille, in

Southern France. His parents worked with the French embassy. They arrived after we did, and I could tell he had difficulty adjusting to this new culture. Given my experience with travel and our combined love for soccer, we became fast friends. There was Rwaida and Chaidia, cousins who came with their families from somewhere in the Middle East. Lucy, my sister's best friend, came from Cameroon. Fatumata was from Mali, Sory from Senegal, and Raphael from Cape Verde. Every kid had a story explaining how this disparate group would find themselves in Guinea-Bissau. There was always a birthday party or event to help bring the community together. It was the most integrated environment that I had ever seen.

For all the good that I saw in Guinea-Bissau, it had its challenges. Unbeknownst to me as a kid, Guinea-Bissau was a true melting pot of ethnicities. Clashes with the various ethnic groups would eventually lead to a civil war that would ensue eight years after we left. Ethnic conflicts resulted from centuries of colonial rule that realigned the Kaabunké territory, what is today south Senegal and north Guinea-Bissau.[80] The government sought to combat tribalism and unite the ethnicities under one rule. However, political opportunists continued to push for ethnic rule that would keep the power in the hands of one ethnic group. The status and income levels would also be transferred to descendants who would carry similar beliefs. The gap between the classes would continue to widen until the underprivileged could bear it no more. Guinea-Bissau is now classified as a fragile state, with institutional instability, low general literacy, and exposure to various types of trafficking, such as drugs or children.[81]

---

80. Lopez and Bartolomeu, "Maritime Safety Administration in Guinea-Bissau : The Marine Engineer's Role in Port State Control."

81. Sangreman, Delgado, and Vaz Martins, "Guinea-Bissau (2014–2016). An empirical study of economic and social human rights in a fragile state",66

With such deep-rooted political and social issues, there are always a lot of guilty parties. The leaders of the Portuguese colonization and the president of the country, João Bernardo Vieira, bear most of the responsibility in this case. The Portuguese claimed Guinea-Bissau in 1446 to serve as a slave-trading center. After Pan-Africanists organized the so-called African Party for the country's independence, multiple coups were unsuccessfully attempted on Vieira's government. The opposition felt that Vieira acted with foreign interests at heart and not the interest of his people. His government's penchant for cronyism, corruption, and its inability to deal with the nation's endemic poverty forced a civil war that would ultimately end in Vieira stepping down.[82] This case study proved that ethical problems persist when leaders do not have the competencies to lead morally and with integrity.

Ethical and Cultural Paradoxes

In the last chapter, we examined how personal agendas can be put ahead of a team or organization's agenda. We'll now go deeper and investigate how leaders can manage situations of ethical paradox. Let's take a look at another case study. I remember only a few moments vividly from my childhood, one being the 1990 World Cup. The World Cup is the only football (soccer) tournament comprised of the best thirty-two national teams. My family watched the games on the edge of our seats from our home in Bissau. That year, everyone was watching one player, Diego Maradona. The electrifying football player from Argentina was participating in his third World Cup. Argentina

---

82. Ciment, *Encyclopedia of Conflicts Since World War II.*

would lose in the finals to West Germany; however, Maradona had already cemented his legacy as a national treasure. Unfortunately, Maradona's life would be marked by drug usage, erratic behavior, and a destructive lifestyle, ultimately leading to his death in November 2020. By contrast, Lionel Messi, Maradona's successor, had not received the same acclaim from his country until recently, when he led his Argentinian team to the 2022 World Cup.[83] The quiet yet captivating football player, who once was a mentee to Maradona, finally has the respect of his people, but the journey to this point was not easy.

Maradona was characterized as this mythical being, almost elevated to a god in the eyes of the Argentinians. They wanted so badly for Messi to be a replica. His skills on the field are strikingly similar to that of Maradona. However, that was the end of the similarities. Maradona's destructive lifestyle was at odds with Messi's calm and quiet nature. Reporter Carlos Reymundo Roberts would say about Messi, "Yes, he is a rare guy. A rare Argentinean: not arrogant, does not swagger, does not talk much, he works hard." Roberts revealed how Argentinians valued self-aggrandizement, which explains why they glorified Maradona, who exemplified those characteristics.[84] Europeans could not comprehend Maradona given his behavior; however, Messi's behavior aligns with European values. Messi has played in Europe since the age of thirteen; the now thirty-six-year-old player has spent most of his life outside Argentina. This paradox adds credence to an undeniable truth—personal values are inextricably linked to cultures.

The Maradona-Messi case presents an interesting ethical paradox

---

83. Brach, "Who Is Lionel Messi? A Comparative Study of Diego Maradona and Lionel Messi."

84. Roberts, "Messi, un tipo raro."

for global leaders to consider. If leaders are expected to be ethical agents, ethical considerations are meant to decipher between doing what is right and what is wrong. However, in some spaces, a leader could be considered a great leader by some despite being corrupt or dishonorable. This phenomenon could be based on culture or popular opinion. Earlier, we talked about followers of destructive leaders. Consider, for example, President Donald Trump, who many US citizens view as a divisive figure. However, in the 2020 presidential election, he would capture 70 million votes in a losing effort, nearly 50 percent of the votes.

The notion of right and wrong has become very contentious and polarizing in American culture and the global community. Ethical issues can put groups of people on two opposing ends. Across cultures, religions, and philosophies, ethics are not as straightforward. The truths that we hold to be self-evident may not, in fact, be so self-evident. Maybe our values require reexamination as well. The question is, "Does the study on leadership matter in a society where even our values are polarizing?" This disconnect drives the need to further understand what defines moral character and how it impacts leadership. Furthermore, this is why any ethical issue requires proper analysis. Let's discuss the role of leaders.

Ethics and Global Leadership

Ethics is concerned with the values and morals an individual or society finds desirable or appropriate.[85] My personal values are drawn from my family, my travels, my lived experiences, and my religious

---

85. Northouse, Leadership: Theory and Practice, 336.

beliefs. All these components shape how I view the world and how people view me. My values define my self-worth and what I assign value to; therefore, in a perfect world, my personal values would align with the organization's values. Many theories have been developed to explain leaders' conduct and character. These theories help to determine where each leader falls on the ethical spectrum. I will focus on three theories: ethical egoism, utilitarianism, and altruism. The three are defined below:[81]

1. *Ethical egoism* states a person should act in a way that brings the greatest good to him or herself. Donald Trump has been characterized as such a leader for acting in ways that promote his own brand. According to a report from Citizens for Responsibility and Ethics in Washington, Trump's refusal to divest from his business while president resulted in over 2,300 conflicts of interest.[86] There may be no better example of ethical egoism. This conflict allowed Trump to take advantage of his presidential network for personal gain.

2. *Consequentialism* or *utilitarianism* is the notion that leaders behave in a manner that creates the greatest good for the greatest number of followers.[87] The Pan-African movement in Guinea-Bissau mobilized the population around a few central objectives, including independence and development. The objectives were made to unify everyone who lived in the territory colonized by the Portuguese. This utilitarian approach was implemented because it greatly benefited a large percentage of the population.

---

86. Bookbinder, "G-7 at Trump's Doral Resort? The Original Sin of This Presidency Is Failure to Divest

87. Schumann, "A Moral Principles Framework for Human Resource Management Ethics."

3. *Altruism* is an approach that suggests actions are moral, and the primary motivation is to promote the best interests of others. Altruistic behavior is most closely associated with servant leadership. It has been best seen in the likes of Mother Teresa or Mahatma Gandhi, people who gave themselves unconditionally to noble causes. Altruism is harder to emulate because it requires a devotion to helping others without pretext.

These three ethical philosophies help explain where a leader may find themself when analyzing their personal interests versus the interests of others. Figure 6.1 illustrates this point perfectly. Ethical egoism contributes to a high degree of self-interest and a low concern for others. In comparison, altruism results in a deep concern for others and low concern for self. Utilitarianism provides a balance between concern for self and concern for others. In summary, making moral decisions can benefit the leader and others, or in some situations, it can be a combination. Leaders should assess where they believe they stand on the ethical spectrum and what can be done to achieve an optimal target.

Many other theories exist that explain how other leaders make ethical decisions. For example, deontology states that leaders adhere to duty when making ethical decisions. Therefore, a leader's actions are considered moral if they have a moral right to do it and not infringe on anyone's moral rights.[83] We might see this with members of the military community. They serve their country first; upholding this duty is considered ethical. However, what would happen if their duties conflict? This conflict could create challenges in timely decision-making. Virtue-based ethics is another theory that highlights the need for leaders to be and become more virtuous human beings. The characteristics of a virtuous leader include integrity, public-spiritedness, truthfulness, fidelity, benevolence, and humility.[88] When adapted from a young age, virtues become values that manifest into actions.

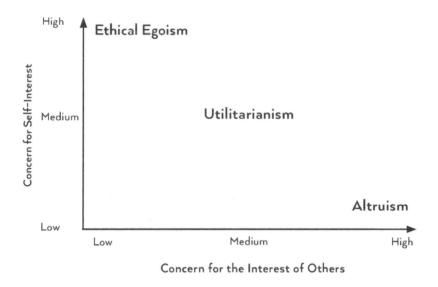

Figure 6.1. Ethical Theories Comparing Self-Interest to the Interest of Others[89]

I identify closely with virtue-based ethics. Virtue, much like a vice, is a form of habit. A habit refers to the tendencies and patterns of behavior or thoughts.[90] For something to become a virtue, it requires time. Virtue ethics theory has been linked closely with studies in theology. For believers in higher powers, it's not merely about being a "good person." For example, a believer in God would say that it's about knowing God and knowing one's God-given purpose on earth and living out that purpose in a virtuous way. If someone were to ask why humility is considered a virtue, a person of Christian faith's response might include a Christian's interpretation of who God is, what God has done, and how God's word

88. Velasquez, "International Business, Morality, and the Common Good

89. Adapted from Northouse, Leadership: Theory and Practice.

90. Fedler, Exploring Christian Ethics: Biblical Foundations for Morality,

on humility has changed them. Morality is a learned behavior that can be fostered by studying and understanding how theological principles apply to individuals, organizations, and communities.

Promoting humility through education, especially at an early age, can prove valuable to individuals and society at large. Failure to foster a community of humble leaders can come at a high cost. A lack of humility can increase feelings of suffering and pain. Therefore, humility has the propensity to create inclusive and sustainable environments in the global context.[91] Humility can also mitigate the impact of pride. When dealing with cultural and ethical situations, pride can contribute to blind spots. Humble leadership emphasizes leading from the bottom and the influence of followers in the leadership process. Humble leadership contributes to positive and proactive employee behavior, as empowered followers are likelier to take initiative.[92]

Integrity is equally as essential to global leadership. People will build trust in a leader who leads with integrity. These leaders are not born with a particular set of essential skills; they spend a reasonable amount of time learning and understanding others. Much like humility, integrity requires bringing personal values into business practices. Global leaders who are consistent and clear with followers, imparting their personal values and beliefs, are more likely to invite followers to model their behavior. Integrity requires courage, honesty, and belief in one's actions. Those who live with integrity will establish an environment of trust with employees, peers, customers, and even competitors.[93]

---

91. Admirand, "The Mind of Christ: Humility and the Intellect in Early Christian Theology by Stephen T. Pardue, Bloomsbury, 2013 (ISBN 978-0-5674-2058-9), Xii + 210 Pp., Hb £65."

92. Chen et al., "Can Leader 'Humility' Spark Employee 'Proactivity'? The Mediating Role of Psychological Empowerment."93. Goldsmith et al., *Global Leadership: The Next Generation*

93. Goldsmith et al., *Global Leadership: The Next Generation*

The Global Inclusive Leadership Imperative

According to the Society for Human Resource Management (SHRM), unethical practices have resulted in over half of the largest bankruptcies in the past thirty years. Enron, Lehman Brothers, and WorldCom are a few examples of corporations that have cost their owners and the economy $1.228 trillion, or almost 10 percent of the US gross domestic product in 2011.[94]

Leadership is an essential element in the pursuit of ethical standards. Leaders should embody the highest levels of workplace ethics within an organization. However, more often than not, leaders are the initiators of organizational moral degradation. In just the last twenty years, members of executive teams have created scandals that have resulted in catastrophic outcomes for individuals and organizations and have had a significant impact on the economy. The potential for scandal is reason enough for every organization to ensure leaders at all levels understand the importance of ethics.

In the earlier example with Maradona, his fellow citizens continued to praise him as a legend regardless of his actions. Messi, who has not fit the image of the traditional Argentinean leader because of his clean-cut and humble nature, had little success drawing his country's support. What is the role of a leader? Is it to act on behalf of the people, the organization, or a more self-serving approach? Leaders must be dynamic in their approach to avoid making unethical decisions. Achieving positive results can also help; in Messi's case, he now has the love of his people without having to change who he is. As such, leaders must ask themselves these questions to help determine the alignment of personal and organizational values:

---

94. Olson, "Shaping an Ethical Workplace Culture."

- Which ethical theory best describes my decision-making style?

- Does this style align with the values of the organization?

- What can I do to ensure my personal values help to morally support the organization?

- What else do I need to do to promote effective decision-making?

When considering these questions, a strategy leaders should consider is undertaking ethics-specific training that promotes ethical leadership through a combination of interpersonal and group activities. Developing team members will ultimately build the model behavior and contribute to fulfillment and goodwill. In the next chapter, we'll explore another psychological phenomenon, motivational factors for leaders.

CHAPTER 7.

Leadership and Motivation

Guinea-Bissau proved to be just what we needed. It was a country at peace, and it was close enough to some of the most jaw-dropping attractions in West Africa. There wasn't enough to do in the country during the months we were out of school, which also happened to fall during the rainy season. The equatorial climate provided enough reason to take extended trips to other countries. In 1992, we got an opportunity to vacation in Ivory Coast, a country east of Bissau. Ivory Coast is widely known by its French translation, Côte d'Ivoire. It's a beautiful country rich in culture and tradition. The country, which received its independence from France in August of 1960, boasts an array of elegant restaurants and cafés, mimicking the authentic Parisian-style bistros. However, so many indigenously cultural aspects were seen in the food, people, and architecture. The food stood out to me the most. I think some of the best acheke, a popular West African dish made of cassava, can be found in Ivory Coast.

We vacationed in Abidjan, the capital city of Ivory Coast, for nearly a month and a half. The city is now dubbed the Manhattan of Africa because of its stunning skyscrapers and scenic views. Back then, the marketplace was equally as impressive. Every type of fruit or vegetable was readily available. The produce was high quality, and even more impressive was that everything was much bigger than usual. I recall my mom's reaction to the size of a mango that could satisfy the whole family. Félix Houphouët-Boigny, the country's first president, was at the center of this social and economic boom. He led the country through decolonization and devised a plan to encourage economic development through agriculture initiatives.[95] His policies led Ivory Coast to wealth for most of his three decades of leadership. He was also well-known for building attractions in his hometown of Yamoussoukro.

Tourists flocked to the Basilica of Our Lady of Peace in Yamoussoukro. We took a trip to see the church the Guinness World Records listed as the largest in the world at 322,917 square feet wide and 518 feet high.[96] I had never seen anything so impressive in my short life. I've been to St. Peter in Vatican City, and as impressive as that structure is, Our Lady of Peace is easily more striking. In comparison, St. Peter is roughly 449 feet tall, visibly smaller than the overwhelming church in Yamoussoukro. President Houphouët-Boigny purposedly wanted to ensure this was the world's largest church. He reportedly spent over $300 million to build the basilica. Everything was done with such meticulous detail. From the 128 massive Doric columns to the enormous dome and a copper cross, every dollar went into making this a centerpiece in the country.

Houphouët-Boigny was beloved by his country, and Ivorians were tolerant of his personal obsessions.[97] However, so many questions surrounded the construction of the church: Why build the basilica

---

95. Cheeseman, Bertrand, and Husaini, *A Dictionary of African Politics*.

96. "The Biggest, Longest, Tallest..."

97. Jenkins, "The Fascinating Story of the Ivory Coast's Mega-Basilica."

in Yamoussoukro? Why build a church for God while there are so many unemployed and near starving? Why spend so much money on the church when funds could be used to solve some of the economic challenges? What was Houphouët-Boigny's motivation?

Many argued that the funds that went toward the construction of the costly project could have helped the country's debt. Moreover, the president could have chosen to build the church in the more populated and modernized city of Abidjan. His camp explained that the church was paid for entirely by Houphouet-Boigny and his sister and was built on land owned by the president.[98] The president saw this project as an experience of faith. He reportedly felt that the blueprint for a great city was a spiritual presence. For Papa Houphouët, as he was affectionately called, that meant expanding Catholicism, the religion he had converted to in his teenage years.[92] In the 1980s, Catholics made up only two million of the total population. The president saw Catholicism as a departure from the tribal and interfaith conflicts that impacted other nations. In his vision, this church would be a pilgrimage center for Catholics of all African nations. However, he built the church in his home country for political reasons. Houphouët-Boigny sought to relocate the capital from Abidjan to Yamoussoukro (Abidjan would remain the economic hub). Yamoussoukro experienced significant construction as Houphouët-Boigny prepared the move.[91]

Some depicted Houphouët-Boigny as an authoritative ruler, but others viewed him as a savior. Susceptible leaders often receive backlash from their decisions. Many decisions that a leader makes have ethical implications. Leaders are entrusted to make decisions knowing that not everyone will agree or benefit from the results.

---

98. Ostling, "The Basilica in the Bush."

Therefore, if we take a step back to understand what drives leaders, we can gain insights into how they will likely make decisions. Leaders' motives often dictate their choices and how they respond to circumstances.[99] Some have altruistic goals, while external rewards drive others. In the case of Houphouet-Boigny, several questions arise that can determine his motives: Was Houphouet-Boigny driven by the desire to memorialize his legacy (as was the practice of many other leaders of the time)? Or did he build the church to create a Vatican-like sanctuary for the betterment of his people? I'd like to believe his motives were pure. Nonetheless, let's explore the many motives that drive leaders and impact their decision-making.

The Motivational Factor

Motivation is the energy that moves people to do what they do.[100] If you work with people, you are likely concerned with what makes them "tick." Leaders are aware of employees' motivations, and employees are equally concerned with leaders' motivations. Examining motivation is a bit perplexing. As seen with Houphouët-Boigny, he had people in both camps, some who understood his motives and others who questioned them. However, the more everyone's motivational factors are met, the more likely organizational goals will also be met. Motivation is drawn from a need. In chapter two, I discussed Maslow's hierarchy of needs, how the theory explains human needs, how they are prioritized from basic needs to psychological needs, and finally, how it explains self-fulfillment of needs. Maslow's research proved

99. Northouse, Leadership: Theory and Practice.

100. Hultman, Balancing Individual and Organizational Values: Walking the Tightrope to Success.

insightful in showing how every human being has needs, and therefore every human being is motivated based on where they are in their life. Our needs may sometimes be part of an unconscious or subconscious thought. When that *need* becomes a *want*, it is a conscious thought.[101]

Motivation is an important topic for leaders, so many theories have been developed to explain the motivational factors that rationalize the needs phenomenon. One such theory was developed by psychologist Frederick Herzberg, who proposed a two-factor theory categorizing motivation into motivators and hygiene. Motivators are the intrinsic factors, such as achievement and recognition, that produce job satisfaction. Hygiene represents extrinsic factors, such as pay, job security, and job dissatisfaction.[102] This theory helped clarify the impact motivation can have on performance and productivity. For example, any offer of employment will provide some extrinsic value upfront. Hygiene factors include salary details, benefits, and work location (especially in a virtual world). An organization might offer promotions or bonuses that satisfy one's intrinsic values to encourage and motivate employees. Whether the motives are intrinsic or extrinsic, the two-factor theory suggests a basis for why and how decisions are made, and actions are taken.

Values and Motivations

In chapter six, we discussed values and their impact on ethical decision-making. Values and needs are both integral to motivational factors. Values are a perception of what is essential in life. In Ken Hultman's

---

101. Adair, Leadership and Motivation: *The Fifty-Fifty Rule and the Eight Key Principles of Motivating Others.*

102. Shirol, "Motivational Factors and Teachers' Job Attitude with Respect to Herzberg Motivation-Hygiene Theory."

book *Balancing Individual and Organizational Values,* he touches on how Maslow's research contributes to the impact values have on our choices. He provides three values that link values to needs:[94]

- *Defensive values* focus on protecting against perceived threats. Examples of needs include security, caution, power, control, and territory. Generally, people who emphasize these values are more concerned with preventing bad things from happening rather than making good things happen. They look to avoid risk and not look for avenues to opportunities. This value can also be used for self-justification to protect one's self-esteem.[103]

- *Stabilizing values* focus on maintaining the status quo. Examples of needs include reliability, consistency, protocol, and procedures. People who fall into this value system emphasize well-being, balance, rest, and relaxation. These individuals resist change and thus have difficulty dealing with chaotic environments or organizational transitions.

- *Growth values* focus on progress or forward movement. Examples of needs include creativity, improvement, innovation, learning, flexibility, and risk-taking. These people emphasize personal, interpersonal, team, and organizational wholeness and integration. The individuals in this group are concerned with self-actualization, the highest level of needs in Maslow's hierarchy of needs.

Values are used to reframe needs in a way that comes across as more socially and organizationally acceptable. Since every leader will have their own value system, the leader must determine if their values are balanced. Balance refers to the degree to which every value is emphasized relative to other values. Balanced values require leaders to

---

103. Rokeach, *The Nature of Human Values*

find an equilibrium between four personal and social needs categories: mastery, a sense of contribution, self-respect, and acceptance. *Mastery* is the personal competence that every leader accumulates over a lifetime of learning, such as self-awareness, self-management, social awareness, relationship skills, and responsible decision-making. *Sense of contribution* is the social competence every leader must have to interact with others, including social, emotional, cognitive, and behavioral skills. *Self-respect* is the personal integrity leaders display to others, acting with honor and dignity. *Acceptance* is the social integrity leaders display to ensure that moral character and social relationships are maintained.[94]

Figure 7.1 displays the balanced value system with the four categories. Although the visual perfectly balances the four categories, this is more for illustrative purposes. The balancing act is based on situational elements.

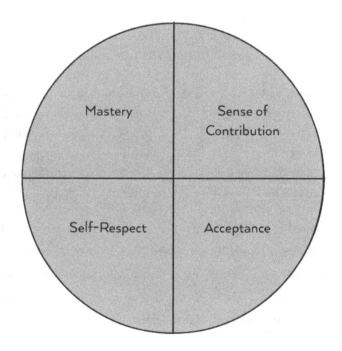

Figure 7.1. Balanced Value System

For example, an organization dealing with team members who feel marginalized may require a leader to display more acceptance. An organization where employees feel like they don't have autonomy in their work may require a leader with more of a sense of contribution. Regardless of the situation, the four value categories are essential for organizational effectiveness.

Motivation and Incentives

Thus far, we discussed how values and needs support motivation. When we talk about motivation, we should also consider incentives. Incentives motivate people to perform. Incentive theory, developed by psychologist Clark Hull, suggests behaviors are driven by a desire for external rewards.[104] Organizations are challenged with aligning strategic goals and individual-based incentives. The underlying dilemma is how to fairly reward followers based not solely on effort but on value created for the organization. To address this challenge, leaders should consider two types of incentives—results-based and behavior-based. *Result-based incentives* are based on outcomes, whereas *behavior-based incentives* are centered on procedures. A bonus can be result-based if the amount of the bonus depends on the employee's performance. A behavioral-based incentive causes an employee to modify their behavior. For example, if an organization is concerned with poor customer service, it can implement behavior-based incentives to improve how its employees respond to customers.

Leaders decide how to reward employees based on the impact the

---

104. Hull, "Behavior Postulates and Corollaries—1949."

employee has shown in promoting organizational change. Similar to the balanced values previously discussed, the optimal form balances results and behavior-based incentives.[105] Leaders should anticipate having to provide both types of benefits to employees. Employees react differently to all situations; therefore, the incentives should be broad enough to address a multitude of needs. Agency theory suggests the problem between incentives and organizational control is a matter of risk-sharing.[106] With any incentive system, there is an embedded risk between the employee and employer regarding the organization's success. Risk-sharing ensures that needs are considered as part of the motivational system.

Leaders must create motivational systems that support organizational goals. To do so, they offer personal pay, skill pay, bonus pay, and profit-sharing. However, equally as necessary are firms' incentives to develop their workforce.[107] In highly competitive business environments, sponsoring training sessions that develop employees incentivizes promotions and overall self-improvement. Leaders and employees who invest in their development gain knowledge and create a reciprocal relationship with the organization, especially when contributing their know-how to information systems.

The Global Inclusive Leadership Imperative

Understanding motivations is not an easy task. It requires leaders willing to take the time to understand who they are and what drives them. This

---

105. Hennart, "Explaining the Swollen Middle: Why Most Transactions Are a Mix of 'Market' and 'Hierarchy.'"

106. Kowtha, "Skills, Incentives, and Control", 55.

107. Messe and Rouland, "Stricter Employment Protection and Firms' Incentives to Sponsor Training: The Case of French Older Workers.

self-awareness will give the leader a clear sense of their capacity, strengths, and weaknesses and a balanced mental and emotional state. Figure 7.2 emphasizes the importance of congruence between the leader's goals, values, and motivations to be an effective and ethical leader. A leader recognizes the business context defined by the environment in which they will operate.[89] However, the environment can not overshadow the need for personal growth and individual motivation.

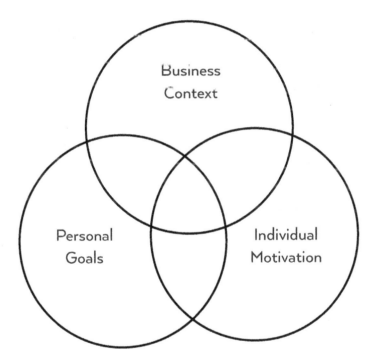

Figure 7.2. Personal and Organizational Congruency[108]

Global inclusive leaders are trustworthy and motivated by virtuous goals. The focus on inclusionary practices can inform how leaders'

---

108. Adapted from Goldsmith et al., *Global Leadership: The Next Generation.*

personal motives will contribute to the organization. Additionally, leaders are challenged with understanding how to drive intrinsic and extrinsic motivations through their organizations. Motivation can be promoted through four objectives:[109] [110]

1. Creating psychologically safe and supportive yet challenging contexts that stimulate intrinsic interest, curiosity, and creativity

2 Having meaningful discussions with employees regularly

3. Allowing freedom of choice within a structure of clarified responsibilities

4. Providing a rationale for tasks and giving sincere feedback in a competent manner that is factual, nonjudgmental, and free from demeaning criticism.

Leaders should ask themselves the following questions to ensure they are building motivation systems for their organizations:

- What intrinsic and extrinsic motivational factors do I find most important? What factors are most important to my team members?

- What organizational incentives satisfy my needs and the needs of my team members?
- What steps can I take to ensure my personal goals align with the organization?

---

109. «Nel, Long. "Theories on character strengths, resilience, hope and self-determination."

110. Stone, Deci, and Ryan, "Beyond Talk: Creating Autonomous Motivation through Self-Determination Theory."

- What procedures, processes, or policies support the organization's motivation system? Are there gaps? If so, what can be done to close them?

Now that we've explored leadership morality in depth, let's shift our focus to the intercultural competencies required to be a globally inclusive leader.

Intercultural Competencies

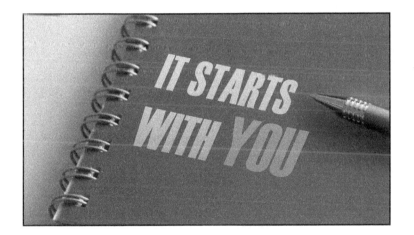

CHAPTER 8.

Building Competencies
for Success

In 1994, my family returned to the US. Our six-year journey had come to an end. The continent of Africa had become home. I felt a sense of belonging, and as soon as I felt comfortable in Guinea-Bissau, we were off to reside in the Washington, DC, area. Although it may have been the end of that period in my life, I knew I would return at some point. I pursued different educational undertakings to help boost my understanding of international relations. First, I took French courses throughout high school and college to keep the basic French I gained over my youth. Then, while completing my MBA, I took a few more classes focused on African politics to learn more about the history of the countries I once called home. Even later in life, during my doctoral program, I focused on global consulting to gain tools to help African economies. Every step helped me get closer to that eventual return to Africa.

In 2012, while working in Europe, I finally made my return to Africa real; my first stop was Senegal. I always felt that my time there was short-lived, and a return would allow me to relive the many things I enjoyed about the country. When I landed in Dakar, I immediately realized I had become an outsider again. Walking outside the airport, the taxi drivers flocked around me aggressively, imploring me to select their ride. They appeared shocked to hear me speak French, expecting an American tourist. Living in the US for so long, I lost a lot of the culture of my previous life in the country. It might have been the way I dressed, the way I walked, or maybe the smile on my face (yes, even a smile is culturally an American feature).

A few friends had accompanied me to Senegal, flying in from various countries. The challenge with having a crowd of friends is that everyone had specific things they wanted to do. However, the Island of Gorée was the one site on everyone's list. To maximize our time, we rented a small inflatable motorboat instead of waiting on the ferry that came every hour or two. We quickly realized that the ferry would have been safer as the boat sailed through ten-foot-tall waves for nearly thirty minutes. We eventually arrived on the dock, welcomed by merchants and street vendors. It was just as beautiful an island as I had remembered before, packed with rich historical elements from wall to wall. We finally came to the Maison des Exclaves (House of Slaves); this was the last dwelling for enslaved people before they were taken over the Atlantic. I stood at the Door of No Return, trying to envision what it must have felt like to be torn from your father and mother and left in utter despair. For many tourists like me, the mood on the ferry back to Dakar was melancholy.

I devoted the rest of the trip to visiting some of my old hangouts, the cathedral, the mosque, and the street markets. Before I left, I stopped by one of the newer but well-known tourist attractions, Le Monument de la Renaissance Africaine (The African Renaissance Monument). The copper structure depicts a man lifting his child and holding his wife by the waist. At 160 feet, the monument is taller than the Statue of Liberty. The monument represents the end of the era of racism and intolerance. Standing before the stunning sight, I was at a loss for words. It was similar to the feeling of first seeing the Statue of Liberty in New York, the Eiffel Tower in Paris, or the Taj Mahal in Agra. Just walking up the stairs provided the elation and exercise I needed. To this day, the symbolic statue represents the aspirations of millions of people to come free from the prevalent bondage of tyranny. In many cases, colonization and various forms of imperialism have prevented many countries from climbing up the social and economic ladder.

After the trip to Senegal, I decided to fulfill another long-time goal and visit South Africa. I had a few friends who lived in Johannesburg, which made the timing perfect. Joburg, as the locals commonly know it, was the most advanced society that I had seen on the continent of Africa. High-rise buildings, beautifully landscaped fields, and decorative pieces of art surrounded the city. One such art structure was the Nelson Mandela statue in Nelson Mandela Square. People stood in lines waiting to take a picture with the towering life-like sculpture. The plaque at the foot of the art piece reads, "Nelson Rolihahla Mandela, A Celebration of Hope 2004 Unveiled by Ndileka Mandela," the eldest grandchild of the late leader. I learned so much about Mandela before the trip, but the opportunity to learn about who he was firsthand was invaluable.

We organized a day trip with a few friends to Soweto, an acronym for South Western Townships, Mandela's hometown. Soweto is only thirty minutes from Joburg. The first stop was the Apartheid Museum. The museum opened in 2001 as a gallery that walked onlookers through the rise and fall of apartheid. When you first enter the building, a sign explains that the admittance ticket classifies each person as White or non-White. Therefore, the visitor is given an experience commiserating with that group's experience. I happened to be placed on the side of the non-White experience, which would leave me in utter disgust for what had been done to those non-White victims. The Population Registration Act of 1950 was the basis for apartheid as it spelled out what required people to be identified and registered from birth as one of four distinct racial groups: White, Colored, Bantu (Black African), and others. Its repeal forty-one years later was a significant step toward ending apartheid,[111] at least from a legislative perspective.

The second stop was the Hector Pieterson Memorial. The memorial was placed near the site where Pieterson was shot on June 16, 1976. He and other school-aged kids protested that the school system forced them to learn Afrikaans and English and did not incorporate their native language, Zulu. The protest would result in multiple deaths as tear gas and, eventually, gunshots were inflicted on the children. Pieterson's death would highlight the atrocities caused by apartheid policies. Millions would see the famous picture of another student carrying Pieterson away from the deadly scene. This uprising would end up putting Soweto on the international map. Although change has come in Soweto, the memorial stands as a commemoration of the South African struggle.

Our final leg of the tour brought us to the center of town, on Vilakazi Street. Vilakazi is most famously known as the street that produced two Nobel Prize winners, Nelson Mandela and Reverend Desmond Tutu. We arrived at the Mandela House, a historic landmark and the house where Mandela lived prior to his imprisonment. The site, also managed by the Apartheid Museum, stands as a heritage to the Mandela family. The neighborhood has since been revamped to include museums, restaurants, and other attractions. It had been quite an emotionally taxing day; we decided to spend the remainder of our time enjoying the local cuisine. Sakhumzi Restaurant gave us a taste of traditional Sowetan food. Not too far from the restaurant,

---

111. Breckenridge, "The Book of Life: The South African population register and the invention of racial descent, 1950-1980."

a local band allowed us to participate in the harmony, playing the instruments and dancing with the crowd. The evening ended on a high note as we embraced every aspect of South African culture.

We now know Mandela because of the impact he's had on the global community. He was instrumental in bridging the gap between Black and Whites in South Africa and creating a model for the world to witness. However, he did not grow up as the leader we now know and love. He was by no means a peacemaker in his younger days. He was by all accounts an angry man, yet he was still devoted to the struggle of the African people. Before his arraignment, he famously said, "During my lifetime, I have dedicated my life to this struggle of the African people. I have fought against White domination, and I have fought against Black domination. I have cherished the ideal of a democratic and free society where all persons will live together in harmony and with equal opportunities. It is an ideal for which I hope to live for and to see realized. But, my Lord, if it needs to be, it is an ideal for which I am prepared to die."[112] His notorious speech was foretelling as he would spend the next twenty-seven years incarcerated. His time in prison changed the course of history as we know it. He grew to embody the characteristics of a global inclusive leader.

I believe Mandela took a sacred journey in prison that propelled him into a global inclusive ministry. This journey allowed him to learn more about who he was and, more importantly, who he needed to be for this world. South Africans (and other countries) use the term *Ubuntu* to describe the innate duty to support one's fellow man.[113] *Ubuntu ethics* is defined as a set of central values: reciprocity, common good, peaceful relations, emphasis on human dignity, the value of human life, consensus, tolerance, and mutual respect.[114] For

---

112. Mandela, *I Am Prepared to Die.*

113. Oppenheim, "Nelson Mandela and the Power of Ubuntu."

Mandela, Ubuntu was formed during childhood but consecrated in Robben Island. In prison is where he had direct contact with the Afrikaner community. This community would include prison guards, warders, and eventually higher-ups who learned from Mandela as he learned from them as well. He would spread the message of equal rights man by man, a monumental task initially, but eventually, he started to get through. The familiarity between the prisoners and guards became evident as tension ceased. He was offered a private prison home; the house would be his last until he was freed.

During his first speech after his release, Mandela affirmed that his work contributed to a greater purpose. He said, "I stand here before you not as a prophet but as a humble servant of you, the people. Your tireless and heroic sacrifices made it possible for me to be here today. I, therefore, place the remaining years of my life in your hands."[115] Mandela would continue to participate in negotiations and peace talks for several years; eventually, the talks would lead to presidential elections, where Mandela would become the first African leader of the nation. In his acceptance speech, he defined how he would rule the country: "I am your servant. It is not the individuals that matter, but the collective. This is a time to heal the old wounds and build a new South Africa."[108] He understood the Ubuntu principle that leaders are leaders based on what they do for others. Global inclusive leaders like Mandela understand the importance of having the requisite tools to lead others. In the following chapter, we'll discuss global inclusive competencies.

---

113. Oppenheim, "Nelson Mandela and the Power of Ubuntu."

114. Ujomudike, "Ubuntu ethics."

115. Mandela, Long Walk to Freedom: The Autobiography of Nelson Mandela

Global Leadership Competencies

Leadership competencies are the capabilities that leaders need to embody to successfully manage their organizations. Global leaders have the added opportunity to manage culturally diverse teams. Figure 8.1 below shows the pyramid model of global leadership.[116] The model has five levels, which together make up the critical competencies of global leaders. The pyramid portrays a cumulative progression of skills from the base to the top. As a leader, understanding where you stand in the progression can provide insight into what training or developmental needs are necessary to advance to the next level.

Figure 8.1. The Pyramid Model of Global Leadership[117]

---

116. Bird and Osland, "Teaching Cultural Sense-Making."

117. Adapted from Bird and Osland, "Teaching Cultural Sense-Making," and Osland, "An Overview of the Global Leadership Literature."

The five levels are described below:

- The first level is comprised of attaining global knowledge. At this foundational level, knowledge is acquired through experiences of working with different cultures, products, processes, and technologies. Global knowledge is a baseline requirement for global leaders as it suggests the prerequisites for team management.[111] Mandela, having lived twenty-seven years in prison, gained this type of knowledge from his interactions with Whites and non-Whites alike. Knowledge can be attained by reading books, listening to podcasts or other media, and through life experiences. Attaining knowledge is the baseline competency for any leader.

- The second level encompasses threshold traits. Integrity, humility, inquisitiveness, and resilience are essential to global leaders. Leaders gain the respect of their followers through threshold traits. As previously discussed, integrity prevents error in judgment as leaders consider all diverse perspectives. Humility averts arrogance and ethnocentrism, which are the downfalls in leadership that assume all answers are known. To be inquisitive is to desire to know more, to be curious enough to ask the right questions. Lastly, resilience is the persistence needed to move forward despite adversity and challenges.[118]

- The third level includes attitudes and orientations defined by a global mindset. A global mindset is a factor of cognitive complexity and cosmopolitanism. Highly cognitively complex leaders are better able to balance contradictions, ambiguities, and tradeoffs[119] and deal with dualities or paradoxes.[120]

---

118. Mendenhall et al., *Global Leadership 2e: Research, Practice, and Development.*

119. Tetlock, "Accountability and Complexity of Thought."

Conversely, cosmopolitanism is an orientation toward the external, advocating for equal consideration. It represents leaders' willingness to engage and explore alternative views held by outsiders.[121] At this level, a leader understands the need to change course, take a different approach, and even take a step back.

- The fourth level includes the interpersonal skills required to work with different cultures, including mindful communication, creating and building trust, and multicultural teaming.[109] Interpersonal skills are another area where Mandela successfully gained the trust of Whites at the highest level of government. He could get to the heart of people because others felt he was looking out for their good. At this level, it's about making the connections that bring about long-term relationships. People who excel here do so because they are genuine in their intent.

- The fifth and final level represents the system skills; these skills are essentially crosscutting skills that allow leaders to adapt to cultural differences and use those differences as a competitive advantage. Some skills include making ethical decisions, leading change, architecting, building communities, and influencing stakeholders. Global leaders are charged with balancing multiple skills. They give people a sense of membership; they create organizational design and structure. And they continuously perform environmental scans to ensure they are always supporting change.[111]

120. Pucik, Evans, and Bjorkman, *The Global Challenge: International Human Resource Management.*

121. Levy et al., "What We Talk about When We Talk about 'Global Mindset': Managerial Cognition in Multinational Corporations

Although the model identifies the building blocks required for global leaders, it does not accurately represent the convoluted journey a leader undertakes, which could alter when the levels come into play. For instance, Mandela may not have had a global mindset during his imprisonment. However, he already possessed the interpersonal skills related to the fourth level. As illustrative as this model is, it's highly dependent on the environment.[111] As such, let's explore another way to examine intercultural and inclusive competencies.

Intercultural and Inclusive Competencies

The proliferation of globalization underscores the need for intercultural and inclusive competency in organizations. Intercultural competence is a skill that gives individuals the capacity to respond in the face of intercultural and interpersonal situations.[122] Leaders require intercultural knowledge and intelligence to effectively serve their organizations. Intelligence, in this context, is defined as the "ability to grasp and reason correctly with abstractions (concepts) and solve problems."[123] Emotional, social, and cultural intelligence are precursors to ensuring teams are equipped to support globalizing and changing organizations. Let's investigate how these three contribute to a leader's toolkit.

---

122. Lundby and Jolton, *Going Global: Practical Applications and Recommendations for HR and OD Professionals in the Global Workplace, 2010.*

123. Hunter and Schmidt, "Intelligence and Job Performance: Economic and Social Implications."

Emotional Intelligence

Years ago, one could argue that emotions had a limited place in the business world. Nowadays, leaders are more prone to understanding how emotions can reveal interpersonal communication. Our emotions are defined by our state of mind, which makes us who we are and gives light to our daily decisions and actions. Psychologist Paul Eckman identified ten basic emotions that he believed are universally experienced in all human cultures. These emotions, he explained, are happiness, sadness, disgust, fear, surprise, anger, pride, shame, embarrassment, and excitement.[124] However, how these emotions are displayed can vary based on the culture.

Emotional intelligence is a skill that allows an individual to perceive the emotional states of others and regulate their emotional state during those interactions. Emotional intelligence helps individuals understand how facial expressions, body language, tone of voice, or physiological reactions translate and give meaning to what someone might be feeling. For example, as I mentioned before, in the US, a smile may suggest happiness or excitement. However, the same smile can suggest a weakness in a different culture.

Research has proven that emotional intelligence can be linked to job performance. Emotional intelligence can be used to predict the degree to which individuals support the organization in reaching its goals.[125] The term "check-ins" is commonly used to refer to ongoing one-on-one conversations between managers and employees about

---

124. Ekman, "An Argument for Basic Emotions."

125. Côté and Miners, "Emotional Intelligence, Cognitive Intelligence, and Job Performance."

work progress, goals, performance, and plan of action. Using these check-ins, leaders can assess their employees' comfort, strengths and weaknesses, and readiness through emotional intelligence.

Social Intelligence

In the past few decades, little focus was placed on getting along with employees. "As long as the job gets done, everything else will take care of itself"—a likely motto years ago for many organizations. I lived by this mantra for some time, focusing my energy at work mainly on performance and less on the team around me. I paid the price of not knowing or engaging with others, which would have contributed to my performance even more. Organizations working locally and globally have begun to appreciate the need for social customs at work. Social intelligence is the skill that emphasizes getting along with others around us through four key components: social interest, social self-efficacy, empathy skills, and social performance skills. Social interest corresponds to one's concern for others. Social self-efficacy is related to feelings of confidence in social settings. Empathy enables one to cognitively understand others, while performance skills are behaviors that stimulate engagement.[126]

Social interaction, especially in virtual settings, can be uncomfortable at times. What makes it so uncomfortable? It could be that the conversation seems to be going in two different directions or that expectations were misaligned. Such interactions point to the need for social awareness. It becomes even more important to be socially intelligent when dealing with people from different backgrounds and

---

126. Cantor and Kihlstrom, "Personality and Social Intelligence."

cultures. A simple way to accomplish social norming is by initiating team-building activities. Inviting team members to dinner with the family, celebrating cultural holidays with team members, or taking time out of the workday are all ways to create an environment where a social relationship can foster organically. Whether through sports, music, family, or religious activities, finding common ground can promote social inclusivity. When no commonalities are apparent on the surface, leaders should look for ways to appreciate cultural differences. When I struggled to find that link, I used it as a learning opportunity. Now, I play golf, bike, and hike, all because I took an interest in creating a connection with a colleague.

Cultural Intelligence

Rooted in the knowledge of intercultural and inclusionary competence is cultural intelligence. Cultural intelligence helps to explain why people behave the way they do. Cultural intelligence is defined as an intellectual understanding of cultures that allows leaders to determine other ways to engage with teams or individuals. Cultural intelligence may not necessarily contribute to building empathy, but it provides the ideal cross-cultural learning platform.[127] Developing cultural intelligence requires a three-pronged approach that includes knowledge, mindfulness, and behavior. According to cultural researcher David C. Thomas, individuals should have a basic understanding of culture and cross-cultural interactions; this is the knowledge aspect. Mindfulness, on the other hand, links knowledge to action. Mindfulness is a heightened awareness of and enhanced

---

127. Schein, *Organizational Culture and Leadership*

attention to everyday experiences.[128] Lastly, behavior ability involves choosing the appropriate behavior applicable to different intercultural situations and extrapolating to generate new behavior.[129]

Unlike emotional and social intelligence, cultural intelligence is typically quickly applied in organizational settings. It is a learned process that will involve training. Most global organizations have invested in some degree of cultural training. However, intercultural competence requires training, coaching, and other self-directed activities such as books, videos, cross-cultural music, art, films, documentaries, festivals, religious events, community interactions, international travel, etc.[130] Culturally intelligent individuals have a quest for ongoing cultural information, and that knowledge changes their perspective and eventually leads to behavioral changes.

The Global Inclusive Leadership Imperative

Leading and engaging with people requires interpersonal and inclusive skills. Without influential leaders like Mandela, change is futile. The character of an organization is defined by leaders who help people first and ensure the products and services offered contribute to the welfare of communities. Great leaders are aware of the changing disposition and needs of the people. Mandela was such a leader. In the book *Leading like Mandela*, Martin Kalungu-Banda surmises that Mandela had a deep sense of awe and respect for human beings. Mandela

128. Brown and Ryan, "The Benefits of Being Present: Mindfulness and Its Role in Psychological Well-Being."

129. Esterhuizen and Kirkpatrick, "Intercultural–Global Competencies for the 21st Century and Beyond."

130. Kalungu-Banda, Leading Like Madiba: Leadership Lessons from Nelson Mandela

would find inspiration in others.[131] Inspiration can be contagious and can undoubtedly find sustenance in an organization. Here are a few questions to ensure global inclusive leadership competencies are present:

• What characteristics of a global leader do I believe I currently possess?

• What characteristics of a global leader do others see in me?

• What traits must I acquire to be a more effective global leader?

• Based on my organization's needs, what skills do I need to prioritize?

There are three approaches leaders can use to ensure they can inspire and build inclusive teams. It's an art form that requires one to be empathetic, inquiring, and engaging with people. The art of empathy requires leaders to see themselves in the shoes of their people. Empathy is a universal quality that allows leaders and followers to engage with mutual respect. The art of inquiry requires listening skills. Inquiry also requires asking the right questions to help form goals. Lastly, the art of engagement requires time and energy to develop relationships. Maya Angelou once said, "I've learned that people will forget what you said, people will forget what you did, but people will never forget how you made them feel." Leaders should possess people-centric skills and must be willing to connect with followers. The next chapter will provide resources that help to assess global inclusive leadership capabilities.

---

131. Kalungu-Banda, *Leading Like Madiba: Leadership Lessons from Nelson Mandela.*

CHAPTER 9

Global Inclusive Leadership Competency Resources

In 2009, while pursuing my MBA at Howard University, the business school hosted President Ellen Johnson Sirleaf of Liberia. Sirleaf became Africa's first female president in 2006. In 2011, she was awarded the Nobel Peace Prize for her work with women in peacekeeping efforts. She reduced the national debt during her two terms and made significant foreign and national policy changes. Being one of the few invited to participate in her presentation and Q and A session was an honor. She spoke so eloquently about the need for the continued inclusion of women in African and American politics, the challenges of reconciling the rights of the indigenous people, and building a post-conflict society.

As I sat there at the edge of my seat, listening to her every word, I couldn't help but connect the dots to a time long ago when I called Liberia home. Sirleaf served as assistant minister of finance from 1972 to 1973 under President William Tolbert. When President Doe, the same president discussed in chapter two, staged a coup d'état assassinating Tolbert and his followers, Sirleaf was one of three leaders whose lives were spared. She would go on to serve as finance minister from 1980 to 1985 under Samuel Doe's presidency. It didn't matter who she served under; she always held the highest standard of personal integrity. She openly criticized both administration policies, a trait that would leave her at odds with both leaders. Under Doe's regime, she went into exile to the US, where she watched the country fall into civil war.[132]

She experienced a number of challenges throughout her political life. She was imprisoned several times for speaking out against corrupt government practices. She lost the presidential election the first time she ran. Even during her time as president, she spent a lot of time repairing the years of misrule done by her predecessors. For example, when she took office, she inherited a massive total of $3.7 billion in international debt.[133] Toward the end of her term, she grappled with her nation's devastating Ebola crisis, which would claim the lives of millions. Nevertheless, through all the challenges, she persisted. As a result, she has an undisputable legacy. Sirleaf broke the glass ceiling and made it realistic for women worldwide to aspire to attain such heights. As I watched her speak with such calmness in her voice, I was reminded of her journey to attain such a level of success.

Unquestionably, Sirleaf is a global inclusive leader. In their book *No Hard Feelings*, authors Liz Fosslien and Mollie West Duffy explain, "Diversity is having a seat at the table, inclusion is having a voice, and belonging is having that voice be heard."[134] Sirleaf was the epitome of a leader who understood the need to belong. She was known as Liberia's Iron Lady, proving that men are not the only ones who can manage the office of the president. She was committed to just, transparent, and productive

---

132. Scully, "Ellen Johnson Sirleaf," April 8, 2016

133. Jet, *Fostering Liberia's Renewal.*

134. Fosslien and Duffy, *No Hard Feelings: Emotions at Work and How They Help Us Succeed.*

leadership. Her presidency would open the door for discussions on African women's empowerment at all levels, from the local to the presidential.

Three key elements to women's inclusion and empowerment at all organizational levels are education and training, practice representing community interests, and support from older role models and political leaders.[135] Sirleaf remained a proponent of education, always ensuring people had access to information and open doors to educational opportunities. I have often heard the famous quote, "Leaders are not born; they are made." The truth is leaders aren't born; they are educated.

Everything Begins and Ends with "You"

Education is the cornerstone of successful leadership. At no point can any leader claim to have all the information needed to make effective decisions; however, educating oneself can provide the skills and characteristics to determine and process all options. The most significant decision is the willingness to invest time and resources in developing "you." Intercultural and inclusive competence training and development can be a massive undertaking for an organization of any size; however, it is necessary for any growth plan. The most immediate question is "Where do I start?" I suggest two starting points in the journey toward interculturally competent teams: a) understanding the need for an intercultural and inclusive environment and b) assessing leadership's intercultural and inclusive competencies. Let's explore each of these further.

---

135. Mikell, "A Woman You Can Trust: Ellen-Johnson Sirleaf and Political Leadership in Sub-Saharan Africa - GIWPS." 136. Northouse, *Leadership: Theory and Practice.*

Understanding the Need for an Intercultural and Inclusive Landscape

It's hard to determine whether an organization and its people are interculturally and inclusively competent. As such, leaders should undertake disconfirmation methods. Edgar Schein defines disconfirmation as any information that shows someone in the organization that some of its goals are not being met or that some of its processes are not accomplishing what they were supposed to accomplish, such as retention goals.[120] This information can help indicate issues that require further evidence to support decision-making. Market trends, political commentary, and employee surveys are all resources that produce the data that leaders require to make changes. Surveys, in particular, can be challenging to properly administer. However, they provide insight that will improve how the organization strategizes and shed light on where they should invest resources. Surveys can also be part of the organizational strategy to uncover quality processes, employee engagement, innovation, and customer loyalty.[115]

Assess Leadership's Intercultural and Inclusive Competencies

A survey cannot help an organization understand the culture; culture-specific assessments can provide insights into the cultural environment. Performing cultural assessments is the next step. Several assessment tools for intercultural competence exist in the marketplace. Therefore, social and cultural intelligence can be assessed using various tools to support the drive toward organizational effectiveness and cultural development:

- Cultural knowledge test—these tests provide insights into intercultural-related knowledge. They are a great test to gauge the level of cultural awareness.

- The London School of English provides an intercultural quiz to assess whether one's cultural skills and awareness will be successful in the global environment. https://www.londonschool.com/lsic/resources/intercultural-quiz/

- The US State Department offers quizzes, scenarios, and role-play that test cultural awareness. https://www.state.gov/courses/answeringdifficultquestions/html/app.htm?p=practice_p1.htm

- Alberta Medical Association provides a self-assessment tool that measures one's diversity and inclusion leadership capability. https://www.albertadoctors.org/Healthy%20Working%20Environments/diversity-and-inclusion-assessment-tool.pdf

- Hofstede Culture in the Workplace Questionnaire (CWQ)—this questionnaire measures personal cultural preferences on six dimensions: individualism, power distance, certainty, achievement, time orientation, and indulgence. The Hofstede CWQ, when combined with personalized coaching and training, is a powerful way to increase one's cultural sensitivity and improve collaboration, business performance, and personal effectiveness. https://cultureinworkplace.com/hofstedecwq/

- The Dimensions of Culture questionnaire—this questionnaire is adapted from the culture questionnaire used in the Global Leadership and Organizational Behavior Effectiveness (GLOBE) studies. Results from the GLOBE project provided an additional lens through which leaders can better understand how to perform well in an international environment.[136] The questionnaire assesses perceptions of various characteristics of one's culture. The appendix includes a reproduction of the questionnaire with mean scores of select cultural clusters to compare attitudes and perceptions of other cultures. Please note that the mean scores represented are used for illustrative purposes only, not for research.

• Intercultural Development Inventory (IDI)—IDI assesses the ability to shift cultural perspective and adapt behavior appropriately to cultural differences and commonalities. https://idiinventory.com/products/

• Cross-Cultural Adaptability Inventory (CCAI) CCAI identifies individual strengths and weaknesses in four skill areas fundamental to effective cross-cultural communication and interaction, including emotional resilience, flexibility/openness, perceptual acuity, and personal autonomy. CCAI can help leaders transition into new environments. Several organizations offer the assessment; I've provided one site as a reference. https://hrdqstore. com/products/cross-cultural-adaptability-inventory

• TASCA Global provides talent solutions for cultural agility. The organization offers different self-assessment tools (e.g., CASA, CAST, and SAGE tools) to gain insight into cross-cultural competencies and proposes guidance to develop those competencies. http://www.tascaglobal.com/assessment.html

• Cultural Agility Self-Assessment (CASA)—CASA is a self-awareness and development tool designed for leaders who need

---

136. Northouse, *Leadership: Theory and Practice*

to succeed in multicultural, cross-cultural, or international settings. CASA is used in various learning environments, such as workshops, training sessions, and as part of talent and leadership development programs.

- Cultural Agility Selection Test (CAST)—CAST combines the validity of an assessment with a structured interview to predict who will succeed in multicultural, cross-cultural, and international settings. CAST is used in assessment centers and selection systems to identify or promote individuals into global roles.

- Self-Assessment for Global Endeavors (SAGE)—SAGE is a decision-making tool for employees to explore whether an international assignment is right for them and their family members. As a private and confidential interactive tool, SAGE covers personality, family and personal life, and career and professional development issues.

- Organizational Culture Assessment Instrument (OCAI)— OCAI provides a unique culture profile that can supply organizations with the fundamental assumptions under which it operates and the values that characterize it. The results of this tool can help create motivation and readiness for change. Therefore, the OCAI is a central component in defining what the members of the organization expect in the future. https://www.ocai-online.com/products

Design a Training Approach Focused on "Us"

The previous section focused on several self-assessments to help develop "you" as a leader. However, you'll need to give your teams of leaders and followers what they need to lead inclusively. Preparing leaders and teams for intercultural competencies requires a training approach to support positive interactions with diverse cultures. In my experience, this requires various types of approaches that appeal to different types of learners. Below, I share three training styles a leader should consider when building a robust, inclusive training plan.

- *Didactic training*—this training method is helpful when information is provided to participants, as is done in a classroom setting. Three types of didactic training approaches are practical information, area studies, and cultural awareness. *Practical information* is the content that focuses on a culture's living conditions, including appropriate attire, language, travel, etc. Area *studies* give insights into the history, values, economy, and political structure of the host culture. *Cultural awareness* can take place in many forms, most notably as a cultural assimilator. A cultural assimilator creates an environment that exposes one culture to another by revealing attitudes, role perceptions, customs, and values.[137]

- *Experiential training*—this training intervention approach focuses on learning by doing rather than *listening* to a facilitator in the classroom-type setting. Experiential training provides practical skills to ease the adoption when interacting with the native population. Role-playing and simulations are ideal experiential training interventions. These methods have proven effective by engaging participants in interactive scenarios that help them understand and respond to intercultural interactions in the workplace. Behavior modification is another type of experiential training based on social learning. This method allows leaders to shape human behavior to conform to the desired standard. For example,

---

137. Kealey and Protheroe, "The Effectiveness of Cross-Cultural Training for Expatriates: An Assessment of the Literature on the Issue."

when employees see rewards attributed to a specific behavior, they are likely to conform to that behavior to receive the reward. Coaching should always be provided to leaders and followers to support positive reinforcement and constructive feedback.[138]

- *Mixed training*—this training intervention takes elements of both didactic and experiential training. This flexibility allows organizations to design interventions specific to the needs of their teams or individuals. Mixed training is typically used with language training, integrated cultural assimilator and behavior modeling training, and relational ideology training. Language is specific to the culture. Therefore, it involves learning the intricacies of the language as it applies to the culture (i.e., English in the US vs. the UK). Cultural assimilators and behavior modeling can be combined as cultural assimilators allow participants to be exposed to a variety of culturally sensitive topics.

In contrast, behavioral modeling provides a space to practice and engage in learning intercultural competence. Another type of mixed training is cultural training based on relational ideology. Relational ideology training combines cross-cultural research with Protestant relational ideology (PRI). PRI refers to a deep-seated belief that affective and relational concerns are inappropriate in some contexts and should be given less attention in work than in nonwork settings. Therefore, this training method allows participants to complete a series of exercises that reveal participants' relational beliefs at work and how those beliefs compare to those of people abroad.[139]

---

138. Black et al., "Behavior Modification in Organizations

139. Sanchez-Burks et al., "Cultural Training Based on a Theory of Relational Ideology."

The Global Inclusive Leadership Imperative

Leaders who develop an understanding of intercultural competencies will significantly benefit their organization and teams. Global inclusive leaders are agile and recognize when and how to appropriately adjust to each cross-cultural situation. Agility is a framework comprised of behavior, psychological ease, cross-cultural interactions, and decision-making capabilities. Cultural agility is the ability to read cross-cultural and multicultural situations. We are all on our journey toward cultural enlightenment. Global inclusive leaders are not perfect; Mandela and Sirleaf had their criticisms. However, they strived for causes beyond their own—noble and moral causes.

Theorist Milton J. Bennet created the Developmental Model of Intercultural Sensitivity to explain how we perceive ourselves and others in the intercultural context. Although the model has yet to be widely tested, it serves as a good baseline for interpersonal and inclusive communication. The theory describes the development process moving along a continuum from ethnocentrism to ethno-relativism. Ethnocentrism includes the act of judging others' cultures, practices, behaviors, and beliefs based on one's own culture or ethnicity as a frame of reference. Ethnocentrism has three stages: cultural denial, cultural defense, and cultural minimization. *Cultural denial* is the failure to perceive different cultures' existence or relevance. *Cultural defense* is a variation where people switch poles so that "they" are superior and "we" are inferior. *Cultural minimization* occurs when people assume that others share their own experiences or that specific fundamental values and beliefs transcend cultural boundaries and thus apply to everyone.

In comparison, ethno-relativism assumes the equality and validity of all groups without judging others by one's own cultural standards. This ability to have more complex personal experiences that led to ethno-relativism views is called intercultural sensitivity.[140] Ethno-relativism also has three stages: cultural acceptance, cultural adaption, and integration. *Cultural acceptance* is when people become conscious of themselves and others in cultural contexts that are equal in complexity but different in form. *Cultural adaption* is the true sign of authenticity when people exemplify inclusive behaviors globally and domestically in all organizational processes. *Integration* is where one's experience of self is expanded to include the movement in and out of different cultural worldviews.[141] Lastly, *cultural integration* comes into play when cultures merge to create new organizational norms and behaviors.[142]

Figure 9.1 depicts the stages of development from denial to integration. As a guide, I've provided suggested training methods and approaches at each stage. As mentioned, no leader is perfect; therefore, we examine ourselves based on what stage characterizes our current state and what training can support personal growth. Additionally, here are a few questions leaders should keep in mind when building interpersonal and inclusive competencies for themselves and their teams:

- What current organizational tools can be leveraged to learn the current state?

- What gaps or challenges can we identify through discon-firmation?

- What do self-assessments reveal about me or my ability to lead inclusively?

---

140. Bennett, "A Developmental Approach to Training for Intercultural Sensitivity."

141. Bennett, *Basic Concepts of Intercultural Communication: Paradigms, Principles, and Practices.*

142. Caligiuri, Cultural Agility: *Building a Pipeline of Successful Global Professionals.*

Ethnocentrism ⟶ **Ethno-relativism**

Judging others cultures, behaviors and beliefs based on one's own culture or ethnicity as a frame of reference

Assuming the equality and validity of all groups without judging others by the standards of one's own culture

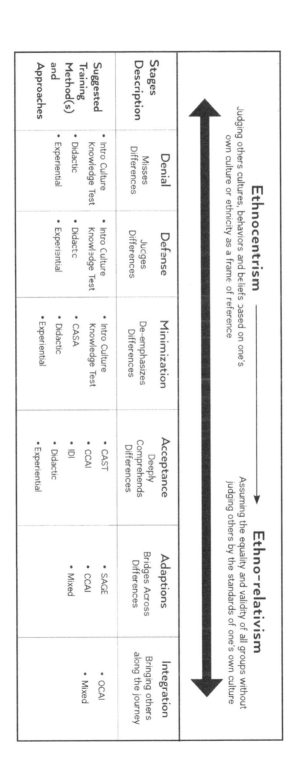

Stages	Denial	Defense	Minimization	Acceptance	Adaptions	Integration
Description	Misses Differences	Judges Differences	De-emphasizes Differences	Deeply Comprehends Differences	Bridges Across Differences	Bringing others along the journey
Suggested Training Method(s) and Approaches	• Intro Culture Knowledge Test • Didactic • Experiental	• Intro Culture Knowledge Test • Didactic • Experiential	• Intro Culture Knowledge Test • CASA • Didactic • Experiential	• CAST • CCAI • IDI • Didactic • Experiential	• SAGE • CCAI • Mixed	• OCAI • Mixed

Figure 9.1. The Developmental Model of Intercultural Sensitivity and Associated Trainings[143]

143. Adapted from "Developmental Model of Intercultural Sensitivity."

- What goals can we set to ensure individual or team challenges are met?

Global inclusive leaders should focus on culturally integrating their global teams to build relationships and networks across cultures. Navigating global environments is a complex undertaking that requires understanding culture, language, government and regulations, and organizational structure.[144] As a result, a global inclusive leader acts as a catalyst, taking in all data points and making recommendations that drive meaningful and transformative insights.

144. Weiss and Khan, *The Global Consultant: How to Make Seven Figures Across Borders*

CHAPTER 10.
_____

Closing Thoughts and
Future Considerations

My experiences living overseas have shaped my understanding of leadership challenges that persist even today. Those experiences provided the ideal background for studies on *global inclusive leadership.* I am convinced that whether it be a for-profit, a nonprofit, or a public organization, *global inclusive leadership* principles are necessary to bring awareness, bridge gaps, and solve the complex business issues of the twenty-first century. Globalization has led to several developments in many societies. Our world is more connected than it's ever been. There are tremendous benefits to working across cultures; however, if history is an indicator of the future, we still have some trials to come. Most notably, leaders have struggled with managing diverse teams. How does a leader account for the needs of each team member while still motivating them to achieve the organization's goals? How does a leader remain mindful of the external environment, and how does that leader's decisions stretch beyond the organization's walls?

These questions are the ones I hoped to address in this book. The global inclusive leader is a mindful leader who understands what they contribute to the team, the community, and society at-large. Globalization has made it abundantly apparent that we can no longer operate in a vacuum; we are all part of a global ecosystem. I insist on the value of inclusivity because, for global inclusive leaders to exist, the first barrier is understanding that everyone must be part of the solution.

The Value of Inclusivity

Every generation is defined by a unifying cause. The advancement in technology undoubtedly defines our generation. Some have suggested that we are on the brink of the fifth industrial revolution, defined by a convergence between humans and technologies. This revolution will certainly optimize human efficiency and productivity.[145] At the same time, we're also seeing a shift in how we engage as humans. Inclusivity has become a cornerstone of organizational culture, with the recent focus on embedding diversity, equity, and inclusion into workplace practices. Leaders must think of inclusivity not only as a strategic imperative but rather as a personal journey everyone undertakes to understand the underlying challenges and needs of the team members. At the start of this journey, each leader looks within to question their motives, aspirations, and ability to lead inclusively.

The lack of inclusion constitutes underrepresentation by certain groups, including race, ethnicity, gender, and disabilities, to name a few. It's incredible what underrepresentation can do to the psyche of a marginalized group. Over the years, there were many times when I experienced a similar feeling of alienation in the workplace. Research has demonstrated that diverse groups are more likely to outperform

---

145. Golic, "Finance and Artificial Intelligence: The Fifth Industrial Revolution and Its Impact on the Financial Sector."

homogeneous groups because they include members with different ways of representing and solving problems.[146] Building diverse teams can contribute to more effective teams and support organizational goals.

Globally, inequality remains one of the pressing challenges in the world system. Global inequality is characterized by economic instability and political struggles.[147] The growing issue of inequality is also apparent with access to healthcare. Most would agree that healthcare is a global human right. Addressing social determinants of health such as social class, ethnicity, occupation, income, education, and gender can prevent the unequal distribution of power and healthcare.[148] Given the magnitude of this problem, global leaders must provide guidance that can help communities and organizations address social and economic gaps.

However, it's important to note that the global inclusive leader should not only be concerned with cross-border leadership. Inclusivity starts at home and in local communities. For example, the COVID-19 pandemic has revealed a great deal about leadership challenges. We've come to understand the true meaning of essential workers as "essential" despite pandemic-related restrictions. What was once a list reserved for police officers, firemen and women, and healthcare workers now included other categories of low-wage workers. Restaurant workers, warehouse workers, postal delivery workers, and many others proved critical for our society to continue. However, most of these workers

---

146. Hong and Page, "Groups of Diverse Problem Solvers Can Outperform Groups of High-Ability Problem Solvers."

147. Ritzer and Dean, Globalization: A Basic Text, 2010.

148. Jong, "Health Inequalities and Migrants: Accessing Healthcare as a Global Human Right."

had the same fears of contracting COVID-19 and continued to go to work to feed their families and keep their health insurance.[149] A leader's responsibility is to the welfare of the community, ensuring workplace safety and fair wages to employees who risk their lives daily.

Morality, Authenticity, and Service

Challenges come in multiple forms, internal and external. At the global level, leaders can help uncover situations with cross-cultural solutions. Values, beliefs, perceptions, and norms contribute to the visible and invisible cultural elements. Dependent on the context, an organization's values can help promote national growth.[150] Alternatively, values can also create economic imbalances and, at times, even support inequalities. There is no basis for universal morality; however, some values or global rights are necessary to ensure globalization does not adversely impact global societies. Such values include temperance, truthfulness, justice, and righteous indignation. Leaders exemplify self-restraint (temperance) in decision-making; they act honestly in all interactions (truthfulness). Additionally, leaders believe in equality and equity (justice) and act immediately in the face of injustice (righteous indignation). The leader brings these values and perspectives to enable global change.

When faced with moral implications, leaders drive organizations with wisdom and intelligence. The leader is expected to deepen their understanding of the moral challenge and lead with a moral compass.

---

149. "Stressed, Unsafe, and Insecure: Essential Workers Need A New, New Deal | Center for Employment Equity | UMass Amherst."

150. Lundby and Jolton, *Going Global: Practical Applications and Recommendations for HR and OD Professionals in the Global Workplace.*

The emphasis is placed on leadership to foster a sense of belonging among members of the organization. This task requires leaders with the highest degree of integrity and authenticity. An authentic leader is genuine, value-based, and original.[151] An authentic leader has five qualities: understanding team members' purpose, practicing solid values, leading with the heart, establishing strong relationships, and demonstrating self-discipline.[152] The global inclusive leader displays authenticity in all interactions.

The global inclusive leader is also an ethical servant. I combine two leadership theories under one umbrella, ethical and servant leadership. *Ethical leadership* is how leaders behave, choose outcomes, and respond to circumstances.[130] *Servant leadership* is about how a leader's purpose will always tie to service to others. A servant leader has ten characteristics, including listening, empathy, healing, awareness, persuasion, conceptualization, foresight, stewardship, commitment to the growth of people, and building community.[153] With all the squalor we've experienced in leadership, the need for ethical and servant leadership is ever more pronounced.

Strategic Planning

Managing people is at the center of a leader's responsibility. However, leaders are integral to developing strategy as well. The challenge for leaders is to drive both people and strategy effectively and efficiently

---

151. Shamir and Eilam, "'What's Your Story?' A Life-Stories Approach to Authentic Leadership Development."

152. George, Authentic Leadership: Rediscovering the Secrets to Creating Lasting Value.

153. Spears and Lawrence, "Focus on Leadership : Servant-Leadership for the Twenty-First Century."

at all levels in the organization. In some organizations, the weighing scale would put strategy and culture at opposing ends of the spectrum, each adversely impacting the other; however, business strategy touches on vision, culture, data, policy, and procedures. Strategy is a critical component requiring alignment and collaboration within an organization. A strategy helps to bring clarity and focus on consensus and decision-making activities. A strategy accentuates the process of agreeing on priorities and implementing those priorities toward realizing organizational purpose. Future strategies will have to include consideration for virtual work, well-being, and the changing workforce dynamics.

The world is rapidly evolving; as a result, leaders should determine ways to move away from traditional approaches and toward solutions for the future. I place great importance on methods such as strategic foresight to help with planning that examines the impact of decisions even ten years from now. Scenario planning is an approach to strategic foresight that helps organizations think through future outcomes.[154] The process allows organizations to understand how they can achieve their goals despite the perceived future challenges or because of future opportunities. Scenario planning is a "participative approach to strategy that features diverse thinking and conversation."[155] Coming out of a planning session, leaders can determine how to achieve their goals despite the perceived challenges. Futuristic thinking can help balance strategy and culture. Therefore, leaders must adopt a future perspective as a way of helping their organizations develop possible future outcomes.[156]

---

154. Canton, Future Smart: *Managing the Game-Changing Trends That Will Transform Your World.*

155. Chermack, *Scenario Planning in Organizations: How to Create, Use, and Assess Scenarios.*

156. Lindgren and Bandhold, *Scenario Planning: The Link Between Future and Strategy.*

Parting Thoughts

I've had the opportunity to learn about many leadership theories that I have mentioned in this book. My research concluded that *global inclusive leadership* is needed for such a time as this. Inclusive leadership causes us to rethink how we can be more effective leaders at home, at work, and in our communities. Additionally, it provides the proper environment for more inclusive outcomes.

The world is experiencing momentous times of uncertainty. As evidenced by the recent pandemic, social and racial tension, climate change, and the political divide, the future can seem unclear. I wrote this book amid these human challenges to guide leaders and future leaders. In particular, I believe younger generations will benefit from reading this book. I hope you found fresh insights and innovative ways to lead for results, build winning teams, and connect with, motivate, and develop employees and constituencies. Lastly, I trust that everyone who reads this book understands the historical context that I shared as it relates to intersectional identities, moral capabilities, and intercultural competencies. I believe there's great optimism if leaders take on globally inclusive characteristics to reach their goals. I look forward to engaging with you all in conversations about this topic. I invite you to connect with me on my website, www.drmutebamukendi.com, or on LinkedIn.

Appendix

Dimensions of Culture Questionnaire

Instructions: Using the following scales, circle the number that most accurately reflects your response to each of the eighteen statements. There are no right or wrong answers, so provide your immediate impressions. (The items on this questionnaire are adapted from the items used in the GLOBE studies to assess the dimensions of culture, but the GLOBE studies used five items to analyze each of the cultural dimensions.)

UNCERTAINTY AVOIDANCE

In this society, orderliness and consistency are stressed, even at the expense of experimentation and innovation.

STRONGLY AGREE   STRONGLY DISAGREE

1   2   3   4   5   6   7

In this society, societal requirements and instructions are spelled out in detail so citizens know what they are expected to do.

STRONGLY AGREE   STRONGLY DISAGREE

1   2   3   4   5   6   7

POWER DISTANCE

In this society, followers are expected to:

QUESTION THEIR
LEADERS WHEN IN
DISAGREEMENT

OBEY THEIR LEADERS
WITHOUT
QUESTION

1   2   3   4   5   6   7

In this society, power is:

SHARED THROUGHOUT
SOCIETY

CONCENTRATED AT
THE TOP

1   2   3   4   5   6   7

INSTITUTIONAL COLLECTIVISM

In this society, leaders encourage group
loyalty even if individual goals suffer.

STRONGLY AGREE   STRONGLY DISAGREE

1   2   3   4   5   6   7

The economic system in this society
is designed to maximize:

INDIVIDUAL
INTERESTS

COLLECTIVE
INTERESTS

1   2   3   4   5   6   7

POWER DISTANCE

In this society, followers are expected to:

QUESTION THEIR LEADERS WHEN IN DISAGREEMENT						OBEY THEIR LEADERS WITHOUT QUESTION
1	2	3	4	5	6	7

In this society, power is:

SHARED THROUGHOUT SOCIETY						CONCENTRATED AT THE TOP
1	2	3	4	5	6	7

INSTITUTIONAL COLLECTIVISM

In this society, leaders encourage group loyalty even if individual goals suffer.

STRONGLY AGREE						STRONGLY DISAGREE
1	2	3	4	5	6	7

The economic system in this society is designed to maximize:

INDIVIDUAL INTERESTS						COLLECTIVE INTERESTS
1	2	3	4	5	6	7

IN-GROUP COLLECTIVISM

In this society, leaders encourage group loyalty
even if individual goals suffer

STRONGLY AGREE   STRONGLY DISAGREE

1   2   3   4   5   6   7

In this society, parents take pride in the
individual accomplishments of their children.

STRONGLY AGREE   STRONGLY DISAGREE

1   2   3   4   5   6   7

GENDER EGALITARIANISM

In this society, boys are encouraged more
than girls to attain a higher education.

STRONGLY AGREE   STRONGLY DISAGREE

1   2   3   4   5   6   7

In this society, who is more likely to
serve in a position of high office.

MEN   WOMEN

1   2   3   4   5   6   7

ASSERTIVENESS

In this society, people are generally:

NONASSERTIVE   ASSERTIVE

1   2   3   4   5   6   7

In this society, people are generally:

TENDER   TOUGH

1   2   3   4   5   6   7

FUTURE ORIENTATION

In this society the accepted norm is to:

ACCEPT THE   PLAN FOR
STATUS QUO   THE FUTURE

1   2   3   4   5   6   7

In this society, people place more emphasis on:

SOLVING   PLANNING FOR
CURRENT PROBLEMS   THE FUTURE

1   2   3   4   5   6   7

PERFORMANCE ORIENTATION

In this society, students are encouraged to strive
for continuously improved performance

STRONGLY AGREE   STRONGLY DISAGREE

1   2   3   4   5   6   7

In this society, people are rewarded
for excellent performance

STRONGLY AGREE   STRONGLY DISAGREE

1   2   3   4   5   6   7

HUMANE ORIENTATION

In this society, people are generally:

NOT CONCERNED   VERY CONCERNED
AT ALL ABOUT OTHERS   ABOUT OTHERS

1   2   3   4   5   6   7

In this society, people are generally:

NOT SENSITIVE   VERY SENSITIVE
TO OTHERS   TO OTHERS

1   2   3   4   5   6   7

SOURCE: Adapted from House, R. J., Hanges, P. J., Javidan, M., Dorfman, P. W., & Gupta, V. (Eds.), Culture, Leadership, and Organizations: The GLOBE Study of 62 Societies, © 2004, SAGE Publications.418 LEADERSHIP THEORY AND PRACTICE

Scoring

The Dimensions of Culture questionnaire is designed to measure your perceptions of the different dimensions of your culture. Score the questionnaire by doing the following. First, sum the two responses you gave for each of the items on each of the dimensions. Second, divide the sum of the responses by two. The result is your mean score for the dimension.

Example. If, for power distance, you circled 3 in response to question 1 and 4 in response to question 2, you would score the dimension as follows:

$$3 + 4 = 7$$
$$7 \div 2 = 3.5$$

Power distance mean score = 3.5

When you are finished scoring, you should have nine mean scores. After you have scored the questionnaire, place your mean scores for each of the dimensions in table 1.

Scoring Interpretation

Your scores on the Dimensions of Culture questionnaire provide data on how you see the culture in which you live and work. Table 1 provides information from the GLOBE project about how subjects from different cultures describe the dimensions of those cultures. The table also provides an *overall* mean for how these dimensions were viewed by people from all of the cultures.

By entering your scores in the last column in table 1, you can get a better understanding of how your perception of your own culture compares to that of others. You can also compare your scores to other specific cultures (e.g., Middle East or Latin America). Do you see your culture as more or less egalitarian than others? Do you think your culture emphasizes the future more than others? Do people from other cultures stress performance less or more than your own culture? Like these questions, the table and your scores can be used to bring to the surface the ways in which your culture and the cultures of others are compatible or incompatible with each other. Understanding how your culture relates to other cultures is the first step to improved understanding between you and people from other cultures.

GLOBE Cultural Dimensions	MEAN SCORE* OF SELECTED CULTURAL CLUSTERS							
	Anglo	Latin America	Middle East	Southern Asia	Latin Europe	GLOBE Overall	YOUR SCORE
Uncertainty Avoidance	4.42	3.62	3.91	4.10	4.18	4.16	
Power Distance	N/A	N/A	N/A	N/A	N/A	5.17	
Institutional Collectivism	4.46	3.86	4.28	4.35	4.01	4.25	
Gender Egalitarinism	3.40	3.41	2.95	3.28	3.36	3.37	
Assertiveness	4.14	4.15	4.14	3.86	3.99	4.14	
Future Orientation	4.08	3.54	3.58	3.98	3.68	3.85	
Performance Orientation	4.37	3.85	3.90	4.33	3.94	4.10	
Humane Orientation	4.20	4.03	4.36	4.71	3.71	4.09	

157. Adapted from House et al., Culture, Leadership, and Organizations: The GLOBE Study of 62 Societies.

*The mean score represents practice scores for selected cultures on each of the nine cultural dimensions. In the GLOBE studies, mean scores were derived from subjects' responses to five questions for each of the dimensions.

Bibliography

Accenture. "The Future of Work: A Hybrid Work Model," April 30, 2021. Accessed March 14, 2023. https://www.accenture.com/us-en/insights/consulting/future-work?c=acn_glb_talentandorganimediarelations_12163686&n=m-rl_0521.

Ackermann, Fran, and Colin Eden. Making Strategy: *Mapping Out Strategic Success.* SAGE, 2011. Adair, John. *Leadership and Motivation: The Fifty-Fifty Rule and the Eight Key Principles of Motivating Others.* Kogan Page Publishers, 2009.

Adler, Nancy E., and Susan Bartholomew. "Managing Globally Competent People." *Academy of Management Perspectives* 6, no. 3 (August 1, 1992): 52–65. https://doi.org/10.5465/ame.1992.4274189.

Admirand, Peter. "The Mind of Christ: Humility and the Intellect in Early Christian Theology by Stephen T. Pardue, Bloomsbury, 2013 (ISBN 978-0-5674-2058-9), Xii + 210 Pp., Hb £65." *Reviews in Religion and Theology,* January 1, 2015. https://doi.org/10.1111/rirt.12457.

Altman, Steven A., and Caroline Bastian. "The State of Globalization in 2021." Harvard Business Review, March 18, 2021. https://hbr.org/2021/03/the-state-of-globalization-in-2021.

Antonacopoulou, Elena P., and Andri Georgiadou. "Leading through Social Distancing: The Future of Work, Corporations and Leadership from Home." *Gender, Work and Organization* 28, no. 2 (March 1, 2021): 749–67. https://doi.org/10.1111/gwao.12533.

Bass, Bernard M. "From Transactional to Transformational Leadership:

Learning to Share the Vision." *Organizational Dynamics* 18, no. 3 (December 1, 1990): 19–31. https://doi.org/10.1016/0090-2616(90)90061-s.

Baumeister, Roy F., and Mark R. Leary. "The Need to Belong: Desire for Interpersonal Attachments as a Fundamental Human Motivation." *Psychological Bulletin* 117, no. 3 (May 1, 1995): 497–529. https://doi.org/10.1037/0033-2909.117.3.497.

Bazerman, Max H., and Ann E. Tenbrunsel. *Blind Spots: Why We Fail to Do What's Right and What to Do about It.* Princeton University Press, 2012.

Bazerman, Max H., and Ovul Sezer. "Bounded Awareness: Implications for Ethical Decision Making." *Organizational Behavior and Human Decision Processes* 136 (September 1, 2016): 95–105. https://doi.org/10.1016/j.obhdp.2015.11.004.

BBC News. "DR Congo: Cursed by Its Natural Wealth." *BBC News,* October 9, 2013. https://www.bbc.com/news/magazine-24396390.

Bennett, Milton J. "A Developmental Approach to Training for Intercultural Sensitivity." *International Journal of Intercultural Relations* 10, no. 2 (January 1, 1986): 179–96. https://doi.org/10.1016/0147-1767(86)90005-2.

Bennett, Milton. *Basic Concepts of Intercultural Communication: Paradigms, Principles, and Practices.* Hachette UK, 2013.

Bilge, Sirma. "Intersectionality Undone: Saving Intersectionality from Feminist Intersectionality Studies." *Du Bois Review: Social Science Research on Race* 10, no. 2 (2013): 405–24.

Bird, Allan, and Joyce S. Osland. "Teaching Cultural Sense-Making." *In Crossing Cultures,* August 2, 2004. https://doi.org/10.4324/9780203218693-12.

Black, Stewart, Donald G. Gardner, Jon L. Pierce, and Richard Steers. "Behavior Modification in Organizations." Organizational Behavior OpenStax (2019).

Borenstein, Lorna. "Three Indisputable Truths About the Great Resignation." Forbes, August 20, 2021. https://www.forbes.com/sites/forbeshumanresourcescouncil/2021/08/20/three-indisputable-truths-about-the-great-resignation/?sh=1b96b1978c93.

Brach, Bartłomiej. "Who Is Lionel Messi? A Comparative Study of Diego Maradona and Lionel Messi." *International Journal of Cultural Studies* 15, no. 4 (July 1, 2012): 415–28. https://doi.org/10.1177/1367877911422859.

Breckenridge, Keith. "The Book of Life: The South African population register and the invention of racial descent, 1950-1980." *Kronos* 40, no. 1 (2014): 225-240.

Brown, Kirk Warren, and Richard M. Ryan. "The Benefits of Being Present: Mindfulness and Its Role in Psychological Well-Being." *Journal of Personality and Social Psychology* 84, no. 4 (April 1, 2003): 822–48. https://doi.org/10.1037/0022-3514.84.4.822.

Caligiuri, Paula. *Cultural Agility: Building a Pipeline of Successful Global Professionals*. John Wiley & Sons, 2013.

Canton, James. *Future Smart: Managing the Game-Changing Trends That Will Transform Your World*. Hachette UK, 2015.

Cantor, Nancy, and John F. Kihlstrom. "Personality and Social Intelligence." *Prentice Hall*, January 1, 1987.

Carino, Meghan McCarty. "Companies Moving to Hybrid Workplaces Will Face New Challenges." Marketplace, April 15, 2021. https://www.marketplace.org/2021/04/15/companies-moving-to-hybrid-workplaces-will-face-new-challenges/.

Center for Employment Equity. "Stressed, Unsafe, and Insecure: Essential Workers Need A New, New Deal | Center for Employment Equity | UMass Amherst," 2021. https://www.umass.edu/employmentequity/stressed-unsafe-and-insecure-essential-workers-need-new-new-deal.

Chen, Yanhong, Bao-Wei Liu, Li Zhang, and Shanshan Qian. "Can Leader

'Humility' Spark Employee 'Proactivity'? The Mediating Role of Psychological Empowerment." *Leadership & Organization Development Journal* 39, no. 3 (April 19, 2018): 326–39. https://doi.org/10.1108/lodj-10-2017-0307.

Cheeseman, Nicholas, Eloïse Bertrand, and Sa'eed Husaini. *A Dictionary of African Politics*, 2019.

Chermack, Thomas J. *Scenario Planning in Organizations: How to Create, Use, and Assess Scenarios.* Berrett-Koehler Publishers, 2011.

Carastathis, Anna. "Intersectionality: Origins, Contestations, Horizons." *U Of Nebraska Press*, November 1, 2016.

Chun, Jennifer, George Lipsitz, and Young Ho Shin. "Intersectionality as a Social Movement Strategy: Asian Immigrant Women Advocates." *Signs* 38, no. 4 (May 3, 2013): 917–40. https://doi.org/10.1086/669575.

CIA. "Senegal - The World Factbook," September 29, 2021. Accessed March 15, 2023. https://www.cia.gov/the-world-factbook/countries/senegal/.

Ciment, James. *Encyclopedia of Conflicts Since World War II.* Routledge, 2015.

Ciulla, Joanne B. "Leadership Ethics: Mapping the Territory." *Business Ethics Quarterly* 5, no. 1 (February 1, 1995): 5–28. https://doi.org/10.2307/3857269.

Collins, Patricia Hill. "Intersectionality's Definitional Dilemmas." *Annual Review of Sociology* 41, no. 1 (August 17, 2015): 1–20. https://doi.org/10.1146/annurev-soc-073014-112142.
Corporate Finance Institute. "Hofstede's Cultural Dimensions Theory," June 1, 2020. Accessed November 28, 2021. https://corporatefinanceinstitute.com/resources/knowledge/other/hofstedes-cultural-dimensions-theory/.

Cormier, Denise. "Why Top Professional Women Still Feel like Outsiders." *Employment Relations Today* 33, no. 1 (March 1, 2006): 27–32. https://doi.org/10.1002/ert.20095.

Côté, Stéphane, and Christopher T. H. Miners. "Emotional Intelligence, Cognitive Intelligence, and Job Performance." *Administrative Science Quarterly* 51, no. 1 (March 1, 2006): 1–28. https://doi.org/10.2189/asqu.51.1.1.

Crenshaw, Kimberlé Williams. "Demarginalizing the Intersection of Race and Sex: A Black Feminist Critique of Antidiscrimination Doctrine, Feminist Theory, and Antiracist Politics [1989]." *Routledge EBooks*, January 1, 1989, 57–80. https://doi.org/10.4324/9780429500480-5.

Crenshaw, Kimberlé Williams. "Mapping the Margins: Intersectionality, Identity Politics, and Violence against Women of Color," Stanford Law Review 43, no. 6 (July 1, 1991): 1241, https://doi.org/10.2307/1229039.

Cummings, Thomas G., and Christopher G. Worley. *Organization Development and Change*. Cengage Learning, 2005.

Costa, John Dalla. *The Ethical Imperative: Why Moral Leadership Is Good Business*. HarperCollins Publishers, 1998.

Davis, Kathy. "Makes a Feminist Theory Successful Intersectionality as Buzzword A Sociology of Science Perspective on What." *Feminist Theory* 9, no. 1 (January 1, 2009): 67–85.

Bookbinder, Noah. "G-7 at Trump's Doral Resort? The Original Sin of This Presidency Is Failure to Divest." *USA TODAY*, September 4, 2019. https://eu.usatoday.com/story/opinion/2019/09/04/trump-presidency-spawns-conflicts-of-interest-personal-profits-column/2197263001/.

Dennis, Peter. "A Brief History of Liberia." *The Center for Applied Linguistics*, 2005.

Domonoske, Camila. "Liberians Vote For Next President, As Ellen Johnson Sirleaf Steps Down." *NPR*, December 26, 2017. https://www.npr.org/sections/thetwo-way/2017/12/26/573482816/liberians-vote-for-next-president-as-ellen-johnson-sirleaf-steps-down.

Ekman, Paul. "An Argument for Basic Emotions." *Cognition & Emotion* 6, no. 3–4 (May 1, 1992): 169–200. https://doi.

org/10.1080/02699939208411068.

Einarsen, Ståle, Merethe Schanke Aasland, and Anders Skogstad. "Destructive Leadership Behaviour: A Definition and Conceptual Model." *Leadership Quarterly* 18, no. 3 (June 1, 2007): 207–16. https://doi.org/10.1016/j.leaqua.2007.03.002.

Engelbrecht, Amos S., Gardielle Heine, and Bright Mahembe. "Integrity, Ethical Leadership, Trust and Work Engagement." *Leadership & Organization Development Journal* 38, no. 3 (April 12, 2017): 368–79. https://doi.org/10.1108/lodj-11-2015-0237.

Esterhuizen, Philip, and Mary K. Kirkpatrick. "Intercultural–Global Competencies for the 21st Century and Beyond." *Journal of Continuing Education in Nursing*, April 28, 2015. https://doi.org/10.3928/01484834-20150420-01.

Fedler, Kyle D. *Exploring Christian Ethics: Biblical Foundations for Morality.* Westminster John Knox Press, 2006.

Feenstra, Sanne, Christopher T. Begeny, Michelle K. Ryan, Floor Rink, Janka I. Stoker, and Jennifer Jordan. "Contextualizing the Impostor 'Syndrome.'" *Frontiers in Psychology* 11 (November 13, 2020). https://doi.org/10.3389/fpsyg.2020.575024.

Fosslien, Liz, and Mollie West Duffy. *No Hard Feelings: Emotions at Work and How They Help Us Succeed.* Penguin UK, 2019.

George, Bill. *Authentic Leadership: Rediscovering the Secrets to Creating Lasting Value.* John Wiley & Sons, 2003.

Gilbert, Daniel, and Timothy D. Wilson. "Miswanting: Some Problems in the Forecasting of Future Affective States." *Cambridge University Press EBooks*, January 1, 2000, 550–64. https://doi.org/10.1017/cbo9780511618031.031.

Goldsmith, Marshall, Cathy Greenberg, Alastair Robertson, and Maya Hu-Chan. *Global Leadership: The Next Generation.* FT Press, 2003.

Golic, Zorica. "Finance and Artificial Intelligence: The Fifth Industrial

Revolution and Its Impact on the Financial Sector." *Zbornik Radova Ekonomskog Fakulteta U Istočnom Sarajevu* 8, no. 19 (February 10, 2020): 67. https://doi.org/10.7251/zrefis1919067g.

Grose, Thomas K. "Wal-Mart's Rollback: After Retreating from Germany, the Giant Retailer Makes a Last Stand in Britain." *U.S. News & World Report*, 2006.

Hatch, Mary Jo, and Majken Schultz. *Organizational Identity: A Reader.* Oxford University Press on Demand, 2004.

Heathfield, Susan M. "Avoiding Ethical Lapses in the Workplace." *LiveAbout*, October 6, 2020. https://www.thebalancecareers.com/did-you-bring-your-ethics-to-work-today-1917741.

Hennart, Jean-François. "Explaining the Swollen Middle: Why Most Transactions Are a Mix of 'Market' and 'Hierarchy.'" *Organization Science* 4, no. 4 (November 1, 1993): 529–47. https://doi.org/10.1287/orsc.4.4.529.

Hines, A. (2006). Strategic foresight: The state of the art. *Futurist, 40*(5), 18-21

Hofstede Insights. "United States - Hofstede Insights," December 11, 2017. https://www.hofstede-insights.com/country/the-usa/.

Hong, Lu, and Scott E. Page. "Groups of Diverse Problem Solvers Can Outperform Groups of High-Ability Problem Solvers." *Proceedings of the National Academy of Sciences of the United States of America* 101, no. 46 (November 16, 2004): 16385–89. https://doi.org/10.1073/pnas.0403723101.

Hougaard, Rasmus, and Jacqueline Carter. *The Mind of the Leader: How to Lead Yourself, Your People, and Your Organization for Extraordinary Results,* 2018.

House, Robert J., Paul J. Hanges, Mansour Javidan, Peter W. Dorfman, and Vipin Gupta. *Culture, Leadership, and Organizations: The GLOBE Study of 62 Societies.* SAGE Publications, 2004.

Hull, Clark L. "Behavior Postulates and Corollaries—1949." *Psychological Review* 57, no. 3 (May 1, 1950): 173–80. https://doi.org/10.1037/h0062809.

Hultman, Ken. *Balancing Individual and Organizational Values: Walking the Tightrope to Success.* Pfeiffer, 2001.

Hunter, John G., and Frank Schmidt. "Intelligence and Job Performance: Economic and Social Implications." *Psychology, Public Policy and Law* 2, no. 3–4 (September 1, 1996): 447–72. https://doi.org/10.1037/1076-8971.2.3-4.447.

Kalungu-Banda, Martin. *Leading Like Madiba: Leadership Lessons from Nelson Mandela.* Juta and Company Ltd, 2006.

Kealey, Daniel J., and David Protheroe. "The Effectiveness of Cross-Cultural Training for Expatriates: An Assessment of the Literature on the Issue." *International Journal of Intercultural Relations* 20, no. 2 (March 1, 1996): 141–65. https://doi.org/10.1016/0147-1767(96)00001-6.
Kowtha, N. Rao. "Skills, Incentives, and Control." *Group & Organization Management*, March 1, 1997. https://doi.org/10.1177/1059601197221006.

Jenkins, Philip. "The Fascinating Story of the Ivory Coast's Mega-Basilica." *The Christian Century*, 2020. https://www.christiancentury.org/article/notes-global-church/fascinating-story-ivory-coast-s-mega-basilica.

Jet. *Fostering Liberia's Renewal*, 2007.

Jong, Floor Christie-De. "Health Inequalities and Migrants: Accessing Healthcare as a Global Human Right." *International Journal of Human Rights in Healthcare*, August 20, 2018. https://doi.org/10.1108/ijhrh-09-2018-076.

Kaelberer, Matthias. "Wal-Mart Goes to Germany: Culture, Institutions, and the Limits of Globalization." *German Politics and Society*, March 1, 2017. https://doi.org/10.3167/gps.2017.350101.

Levy, Orly, Schon Beechler, Sully Taylor, and Nakiye Avdan Boyacıgiller.

"What We Talk about When We Talk about 'Global Mindset': Managerial Cognition in Multinational Corporations." *Journal of International Business Studies* 38, no. 2 (March 21, 2007): 231–58. https://doi.org/10.1057/palgrave. jibs.8400265.

Lindgren, M., and H. Bandhold. *Scenario Planning: The Link Between Future and Strategy.* Springer, 2003.

Lipman-Blumen, Jean. *The Allure of Toxic Leaders: Why We Follow Destructive Bosses and Corrupt Politicians--and How We Can Survive Them.* Oxford University Press, USA, 2006.

Lopez, Gomes, and Anselmo Bartolomeu. "Maritime Safety Administration in Guinea-Bissau : The Marine Engineer's Role in Port State Control." *World Maritime University Dissertations,* January 1, 1999.
Lundby, Kyle, and Jeffrey Jolton. *Going Global: Practical Applications and Recommendations for HR and OD Professionals in the Global Workplace.* John Wiley & Sons, 2010.

Maina, Julius, and Kagure Gacheche. "Conflict in the DRC: 5 Articles That Explain What's Gone Wrong." The Conversation, November 25, 2022. https://theconversation.com/conflict-in-the-drc-5-articles-that-explain-whats-gone-wrong-195332.

Mandela, Nelson. *I Am Prepared to Die.* Imported Publication, 1979.

Mandela, Nelson. *Long Walk to Freedom: The Autobiography of Nelson Mandela.* Hachette UK, 2008.
Marsh, Nick, Mike McAllum, and Dominique Purcell. *Strategic Foresight: The Power of Standing in the Future,* 2002.

McLeod, Saul. "Maslow's Hierarchy of Needs." *Simply Psychology* 1, no. 1–18 (2007).

Mendenhall, Mark E., Joyce Osland, Allan Bird, Gary R. Oddou, Martha L Maznevski, Michael Stevens, and Günter K. Stahl. *Global Leadership 2e: Research, Practice, and Development.* Routledge, 2017.

Mendenhall, Mark E., B. Sebastian Reiche, Allan Bird, and Joyce S. Osland. "Defining the 'Global' in Global Leadership." *Journal of World Business* 47, no. 4 (October 1, 2012): 493–503. https://doi.org/10.1016/j.jwb.2012.01.003.

Messe, Pierre-Jean, and Bénédicte Rouland. "Stricter Employment Protection and Firms' Incentives to Sponsor Training: The Case of French Older Workers." *Labour Economics* 31 (December 1, 2014): 14–26. https://doi.org/10.1016/j.labeco.2014.07.004.

Mikell, Gwendolyn. "A Woman You Can Trust: Ellen-Johnson Sirleaf and Political Leadership in Sub-Saharan Africa - GIWPS." *GIWPS*, October 24, 2009. https://giwps.georgetown.edu/resource/a-woman-you-can-trust-ellen-johnson-sirleaf-and-political-leadership-in-sub-saharan-africa/.

Milken Institute and The Harris Poll. "Global Priorities According to Global Citizens." The Listening Project, October 12, 2020. Accessed March 13, 2023. https://milkeninstitute.org/sites/default/files/reports-pdf/The-Listening-Project_Exec-Summary_v10_0.pdf.

Mount, Portia, and Susan Tardanico. *Beating the Impostor Syndrome.* Center for Creative Leadership, 2014.

Nel, Long. "Theories on character strengths, resilience, hope and self-determination." Toward flourishing: Contextualising positive psychology. Pretoria, South Africa: Van Schaik (2014): 115-140. Lopes, C., 1999. Kaabundé – Espaço, território e poder na Guiné – Bissau, Gâmbia e Casamance pré – coloniais. Afrontamento, Porto

Nielsen, Morten, Jan H. Christensen, Live Bakke Finne, and Stein Knardahl. "Workplace Bullying, Mental Distress, and Sickness Absence: The Protective Role of Social Support." *International Archives of Occupational and Environmental Health* 93, no. 1 (January 1, 2020): 43–53. https://doi.org/10.1007/s00420-019-01463-y.

Northouse, Peter Guy. *Leadership: Theory and Practice.* Sage Publications, 2021.

O'Brien, Gael. "Mark Hurd's Leadership Failure." Business Ethics, November 14, 2010. https://business-ethics.com/2010/08/07/4535-mark-hurds-leadership-failure/.

Office of the Historian. "Foreign Relations of the United States, 1964–1968, Volume XXIII, Congo, 1960–1968 - Office of the Historian." Accessed October 30, 2021. https://history.state.gov/historicaldocuments/frus1964-68v23/d1.

Olson, Stephen D. "Shaping an Ethical Workplace Culture." Society for Human Resource Management, 2013.

Osland, Joyce S. "An Overview of the Global Leadership Literature." *Global Leadership* 2e (March 1, 2013): 52 -91. https://doi.org/10.4324/9780203817865-10.
Ostling, Richard N. "The Basilica in the Bush." TIME.com, June 24, 2001. https://content.time.com/time/magazine/article/0,9171,152145,00.html.

Oppenheim, Claire E. "Nelson Mandela and the Power of Ubuntu." *Religions* 3, no. 2 (April 26, 2012): 369–88. https://doi.org/10.3390/rel3020369.
Padilla, Art, Robert Hogan, and Robert B. Kaiser. "The Toxic Triangle: Destructive Leaders, Susceptible Followers, and Conducive Environments." *Leadership Quarterly* 18, no. 3 (June 1, 2007): 176–94. https://doi.org/10.1016/j.leaqua.2007.03.001.

Perla, Héctor. "Heirs of Sandino." *Latin American Perspectives* 36, no. 6 (November 1, 2009): 80–100. https://doi.org/10.1177/0094582x09350765.

Pucik, Evans, and Bjorkman. *The Global Challenge: International Human Resource Management*, 2016.

Reyntjens, Filip. "The Great African War: Congo and Regional Geopolitics, 1996-2006." *Choice Reviews Online* 47, no. 09 (May 1, 2010): 47–5300. https://doi.org/10.5860/choice.47-5300.

Ritzer, George, and Paul Dean. *Globalization: A Basic Text*. John Wiley & Sons, 2010.

Roberson, Quinetta M. "Disentangling the Meanings of Diversity and Inclusion in Organizations." *Group & Organization Management* 31, no. 2 (April 1, 2006): 212–36. https://doi.org/10.1177/1059601104273064.

Roberts, Carlos M. Reymundo. "Messi, un tipo raro." LA NACION, April 27, 2010. https://www.lanacion.com.ar/deportes/messi-un-tipo-raro-nid1258771/.

Rokeach, Milton. *The Nature of Human Values.* New York : Free Press, 1973.

Sabbott. "Developmental Model of Intercultural Sensitivity." Organizing Engagement, June 9, 2022. https://organizingengagement.org/models/developmental-model-of-intercultural-sensitivity/.
Said, Edward W. "Traveling Theory (1982)." *World Literature in Theory*, 2014, 114–33.

Sanchez-Burks, Jeffrey, Fiona Lee, Richard E. Nisbett, and Oscar Ybarra. "Cultural Training Based on a Theory of Relational Ideology." *Basic and Applied Social Psychology* 29, no. 3 (December 5, 2007): 257–68. https://doi.org/10.1080/01973530701503184.
Sangreman, Carlos, Fátima Delgado, and Luis Vaz Martins. "Guinea-Bissau (2014–2016). An empirical study of economic and social human rights in a fragile state." *Adv. Soc. Sci. Res. J* 5 (2018): 66-84.

Schein, Edgar H. Organizational Culture and Leadership (Jossey-Bass Business & Management Series). Jossey Bass Incorporated, 2004.

Schein, Edgar H. Organizational Culture and Leadership. John Wiley & Sons, 2010.

Schumann, Paul. "A Moral Principles Framework for Human Resource Management Ethics." *Human Resource Management Review* 11, no. 1–2 (March 1, 2001): 93–111. https://doi.org/10.1016/s1053-4822(00)00042-5.

Scully, Pamela. "Ellen Johnson Sirleaf." *Ohio University Press*, April 8, 2016. https://doi.org/10.2307/j.ctv224ttfd.

Sendjaya, Sen. "Morality and Leadership: Examining the Ethics of Transformational Leadership." *Journal of Academic Ethics* 3, no. 1 (November 11, 2005): 75–86. https://doi.org/10.1007/s10805-005-0868-7.

Shamir, Boas, and Galit Eilam. "'What's Your Story?' A Life-Stories Approach to Authentic Leadership Development." *Leadership Quarterly* 16, no. 3 (June 1, 2005): 395–417. https://doi.org/10.1016/j.leaqua.2005.03.005.

Sher, Ehrenhalt A., and Jonathan Englert. "Finance Digital Transformation: Predictions for 2025." Deloitte, July 18, 2020. Accessed March 14, 2023. https://www2.deloitte.com/global/en/pages/finance/articles/gx-finance-digital-transformation-for-cfos.html.
Shiftbalance. "The Story of Me, Us, Now," March 4, 2017. https.//www.youtube.com/watch?v=FgwGgKWqPm8.

Shirol, Sheetal. "Motivational Factors and Teachers' Job Attitude with Respect to Herzberg Motivation-Hygiene Theory." *Journal on Educational Technology* 4, no. 1 (June 1, 2014): 1–5. http://www.indianjournals.com/ijor.aspx?target=ijor:tle&volume=4&issue=1&article=001&type=pdf.

Shore, Lynn M., Amy E. Randel, Beth G. Chung, Michelle Dean, Karen Holcombe Ehrhart, and Gangaram Singh. "Inclusion and Diversity in Work Groups: A Review and Model for Future Research." *Journal of Management* 37, no. 4 (July 1, 2011): 1262–89. https://doi.org/10.1177/0149206310385943.

Simon, Herbert A. *Reason in Human Affairs*. Stanford University Press, 1990.

Sosik, John J., and Dongil Jung. *Full Range Leadership Development: Pathways for People, Profit, and Planet*. Routledge, 2018.

Spears, Larry D., and Michele Lawrence. "Focus on Leadership : Servant-Leadership for the Twenty-First Century." *J. Wiley & Sons EBooks*, January 1, 2002. https://ci.nii.ac.jp/ncid/BA62763151.

Spreitzer, Gretchen M., Morgan W. McCall, and Joan Mahoney. "Early Identification of International Executive Potential." *Journal of Applied*

Psychology 82, no. 1 (February 1, 1997): 6–29. https://doi.org/10.1037/0021-9010.82.1.6.

Stewart, Abigail J., and Christa McDermott. "Gender in Psychology." *Annual Review of Psychology* 55, no. 1 (January 12, 2004): 519–44. https://doi.org/10.1146/annurev.psych.55.090902.141537.

Stone, Dan, Edward L. Deci, and Richard M. Ryan. "Beyond Talk: Creating Autonomous Motivation through Self-Determination Theory." *Journal of General Management* 34, no. 3 (March 1, 2009): 75–91. https://doi.org/10.1177/030630700903400305.

Tapper, James. "Quiet Quitting: Why Doing the Bare Minimum at Work Has Gone Global." *The Guardian*, August 6, 2022. https://www.theguardian.com/money/2022/aug/06/quiet-quitting-why-doing-the-bare-minimum-at-work-has-gone-global.

Tetlock, Philip E. "Accountability and Complexity of Thought." *Journal of Personality and Social Psychology* 45, no. 1 (July 1, 1983): 74–83. https://doi.org/10.1037/0022-3514.45.1.74.

The Guardian. "The Biggest, Longest, Tallest...," September 23, 2020. https://www.theguardian.com/artanddesign/2004/jun/17/architecture.

Thomas, David. "Domain and Development of Cultural Intelligence." *Group & Organization Management* 31, no. 1 (February 1, 2006): 78–99. https://doi.org/10.1177/1059601105275266.

Transparency International. "Seize Mobutu's Wealth or Lose Your Own Money, Western Governments Told - Press." Transparency.org, April 7, 2020. https://www.transparency.org/en/press/seize-mobutus-wealth-or-lose-your-own-money-western-governments-told-1.

Velasquez, Manuel. "International Business, Morality, and the Common Good." *Business Ethics Quarterly* 2, no. 1 (February 1, 1992): 27–40. https://doi.org/10.2307/3857220.

Vinck, Patrick, Phuong Pham, and Tino Kreutzer. "Talking Peace: A Population-Based Survey on Attitudes About Security, Dispute Resolution, and

Post-Conflict Reconstruction in Liberia." *Social Science Research Network*, June 1, 2011. https://doi.org/10.2139/ssrn.1874025.

Walton, Gregory M., and Geoffrey L. Cohen. "A Question of Belonging: Race, Social Fit, and Achievement." *Journal of Personality and Social Psychology* 92, no. 1 (January 1, 2007): 82–96. https://doi.org/10.1037/0022-3514.92.1.82.

Wack, Henry Wellington. *The Story of the Congo Free State: Social, Political, and Economic Aspects of the Belgian System of Government in Central Africa*, 1970.

Weiss, Alan, and Omar Khan. *The Global Consultant: How to Make Seven Figures Across Borders*. Wiley, 2008.

World Economic Forum. "Why the World in 2015 Faces a Leadership Crisis," May 20, 2022. https://www.weforum.org/agenda/2014/11/world-2015-faces-leadership-crisis/.
Ujomudike, Philip Ogochukwu. "Ubuntu ethics." *Encyclopedia of Global Bioethics* (2016): 2869-2881.

Xu, Angela J., Raymond Loi, and Hang-Yue Ngo. "Ethical Leadership Behavior and Employee Justice Perceptions: The Mediating Role of Trust in Organization." *Journal of Business Ethics* 134, no. 3 (March 1, 2016): 493–504. https://doi.org/10.1007/s10551-014-2457-4.

Index

A

Agency theory, 98
Altruism, 85
Automation, 12
Authenticity, 18, 136-137

B

Belonging 25-29, 121
Belonging Uncertainty, 27
Bounded Ethicality, 75
  Bounded Awareness, 75
  Bounded Rationality, 74
  Focalism, 74

C

Conducive Environment (The Toxic Triangle), 70
Cross-Cultural Adaptability Inventory (CCAI), 125
Cultural Agility, 129
Cultural Agility Selection Test (CAST), 126
Cultural Agility Self-Assessment (CASA), 125-126
Cultural Knowledge Test, 124
Cultural Intersectionalist, 46-47
Culture, 48-49, 53-61, 73-77
  Dimensions of Culture, Cultural Dimensions, 41-44
  Types, 42-44

D

Destructive Leader (The Toxic Triangle), 69-70
Developmental Model of Intercultural Sensitivity, 129-131
Dimensions of Culture questionnaire, Appendix

Diversity, 121, 134

E

Ethical Egoism, 84
Ethics
  Behavior, 72-75
  Theory, 84-86
Ethnocentrism, 112, 129
  Cultural Denial, 129
  Cultural Defense, 129
  Cultural Minimization, 129
Ethno-relativism, 129-130
  Cultural Acceptance, 130
  Cultural Adaption, 130
  Integration, 130
Equity, 134, 136
Exclusion, 21-22, 47

G

Globalization, 10-11, 114, 133, 146
Global Inclusive Leadership defined, 17-20
Global Leadership, 12-14, 83, 87
  The Pyramid Model of Global Leadership, 111-114

H

Hofstede Culture in the Workplace Questionnaire (CWQ), 124
Humility, 85-86, 94-95, 112

I

Imposter Syndrome, 24
Inclusion, lack thereof, 9, 15-16, 21,25,27,47,121, 134
Incentives Theory, 97-98

Results-based, 97
Behavior-based, 97
Intercultural Competencies, 17, 19,
127-132
Intercultural Development Inventory (IDI),
125
Intelligence, 114-118
Emotional, 115
Cultural, 116-117
Social, 117-118
Intersectional Identities, Intersectionality,
17, 26, 38-47
Integration, 27, 130
Cross- Cultural, 6
Integrity, 85, 87, 96, 112

L

Leadership
Ethical, 19,76, 89, 145
Inclusive, 15, 139
Leadership Today, /
Pseudo-transformational, 68-69
Servant, 2, 93, 137

M

Moral Capacities, morality, 17, 19, 87,
136
Motivation, 93-101
Motivational System, 98

O

Organizational Development, 53, 58-61
Outsider Syndrome, 23-24

P

Protestant relational ideology (PRI),
128

S

Self-Assessment for Global Endeavors
(SAGE), 126
Strategic Planning, 137
Susceptible follower (The Toxic
Triangle), 70

T

TASCA Global, 125
Training, 126-130
Didactic, 127
Experiential, 127-128
Mixed, 128
Two-Factor theory, 94

U

Ubuntu Ethics, 110
Utilitarianism, 84
Values, 94-97
Balanced Values System, 95-96
Defensive, 95
Growth, 95
Stabilizing, 95

V

Virtue-Based Ethics, 85-86

About the Author

DR. MUTEBA MUKENDI is a second-generation American who spent most of his formative life growing up in the US and different African countries. His travels, which include time spent in Liberia, Senegal, the Democratic Republic of Congo, and Guinea-Bissau, have given him insights into leadership and its intersection with culture and strategy. He's lived and worked abroad in Switzerland and has done a few stints in Brazil, further expanding his broad perspective on organizational cultures, values, and group dynamics. He continued to grow his interest in leadership by completing his doctorate in strategic leadership, focusing on global leadership and ethics. He also holds a master's in business administration and a bachelor's degree in economics.

CPSIA information can be obtained
at www.ICGtesting.com
Printed in the USA
LVHW011321170723
752376LV00003B/231

9 798888 240144